Tips II

More Ideas for Actors

by Jon Jory

CAREER DEVELOPMENT SERIES

A Smith and Kraus Book

A Smith and Kraus Book
Published by Smith and Kraus, Inc.
177 Lyme Road, Hanover, New Hampshire, 03755
www.SmithKraus.com

Manufactured in the United States of America
Text Design by Julia Hill Gignoux

First Edition: December 2004
10 9 8 7 6 5 4 3 2 1

The Library of Congress Cataloging-In-Publication Data
Provided by Quality Books, Inc.
Jory, Jon.
Tips for actors / by Jon Jory —1st ed.
p. cm. — (Career development series)
ISBN 1-57525-202-3(vol.1) ISBN 1-57525-323-2 (vol.2)
1. Acting. I. Title. III. Series.
PN2061.J67 2000   792'.028
QBI00-294

Contents

To Jessica, Victor, and Miranda

Preface

If you think of the great acting theorists as architects, then this acting book is by a carpenter. Although the art of acting must be complexly addressed and is an intellectual, spiritual, and emotional discipline, there are a number of simple things to say about it. Hopefully, this book says some of them.

The tips work two ways. They remind you of necessities you have overlooked while you're trying to accomplish something else: My view is that simply because something is self-evident doesn't ensure you recognize it in the heat of battle. They also deal with small parts of larger problems, and this gives you a place to start without being overwhelmed by the big picture. Tips are, in fact, shortcuts while pursuing larger game.

In other words, this is a book of reductionist thinking about acting that attempts to give you, or remind you of, small tools for whittling this profound art of acting down to a size you feel comfortable coping with. It's a big deal to confront a grizzly bear in the woods; however, if you knew a bunch of smaller things—such as walking slowly backward while maintaining eye contact—you would probably survive the encounter. That, in my opinion, is a tip. You don't need to know everything about grizzly bears to employ the tip and benefit from it; it's something that works for that situation. These tips won't explain the bear, but they'll help get you out alive.

Jon Jory

BASICS

CIRCUMSTANCES

These are no subjective opinions. These are facts in the text. It is six o'clock. It takes place in Las Vegas. Jack is a butcher, etc. Sit down and list them. Then ask questions of yourself to break them open. It says Bethany had an abortion. Ask why. Ask if religion affects her choice. Ask if anyone influenced her choice. Ask whatever strikes you as pertinent. Answer and ask again until it creates a lake of information you can draw on in rehearsal. To break open a single circumstance may take a half hour, so pick the most pertinent to work on if your time is limited. This is crucial work. If you don't understand the circumstances, you can't build the role appropriately or understand the rules of the text. Acting serves the text, and the text gives boundaries to the actor. Let's call these boundaries the rules. The circumstances are the rules for that particular play. We need the rules to do the work.

BEATS

The beat is to acting as the paragraph is to writing. The beat changes when the subject (textual or subtextual) changes. The beat is ordinarily defined not from your character's viewpoint but from the text's. Beats are ordinarily marked by the actor with brackets [ ]. The uses of marking the beats are many. It forces us to ask what is really going on before we can identify it. It helps us understand the text's rhythm and style as it would in music. It points out that a transition exists and must be played between beats. It gives us units of text that we can further analyze for context and structure. It makes clear when the action changes. Sometimes a beat may seem to be about going shopping but is really about the characters' relationship on a subtextual level. The beat then ends when the subtext changes. Beats strung end to end with different actions, obstacles, and tactics identified create the role's landscape.

AN ACTION

Whole tomes are written on the action. Whole theories make it central. Every actor claims to use them. Why then do they seem so often absent? To remind us, the action is either what you want the other person onstage to do, to feel, or to understand. If you're alone onstage, the action has the same definition only applied to you. Because large roles are made up of hundreds of actions, very few performers will do all that homework. Admit you are lazy and use them for spot work. This moment isn't working—what's the action? This beat seems unclear—what's the action? I feel self-conscious here—what's the action? For an action to be dramatic, it needs a counterbalancing obstacle; so make sure you know what it is. When you know the action and the obstacle and it still isn't working, raise the stakes. Simple as that.

ACTION II

This action: What you want the other to do, feel, or understand, hopefully puts the scene *between* you. The action probably relates to the meaning of the scene or the theme of the play. If the action of the beat is "I want him to kiss me," that's good because you will know when the action is completed. If, however, the action oversimplifies the intent of the moment, it will demean the scene. To further pursue the idea of the action, use the words "to what end?" The answer to the question "I want him to kiss me, but to what end?" (nothing bawdy, please) will add a resonance to the acting. In a sense, every action contains philosophy and poetry; it is not simply the pursuit of a "square meal." By understanding not only the action's simplicity but its resonance, the acting will have weight and dimension. No action is graven in stone. You can try it and then change it. The action isn't a "result"; it's an attempt. But have one.

TACTICS

The action is what your character wants another character to do. The tactic is how you get the other to do it. The action, as in Lopahin trying to get Madam Ranevskaya to sell the cherry orchard, may last for an entire play, but the tactics keep changing. The same thing is true in a single beat. Even in six lines there may be several changes of tactics. You may cajole, play on her sympathy, demand, and sulk all on a single page in the service of a single need. The more difficult the obstacle, the greater the number of tactics. The values to the actor of varying the tactics are many. On the simplest level, it provides crucial variety, which *is* the staff of life for both the actor and the audience. Needing to change tactics is the sign of a good, juicy, frustrating obstacle that engages our full attention. Each change of tactic also provokes a new and different response from our scene partner, which moves the scene forward. One warning: Make sure the tactics are appropriate to the character and to your commonsense view of what people actually do in real circumstances.

SUBTEXT

Subtext is, obviously, what you really mean under what you say. You say, "I'm going to bed"; you mean "I don't want to talk to you." Over the course of a career as a director, I've found that asking what the subtext is improves work more immediately than almost any other tool. Usually when you identify the subtext, you find it also describes an action and thus is doubly useful. While most actors use subtext consciously or unconsciously, they may not think to decode the *other* characters' unspoken intentions, which can unlock a recalcitrant scene. We not only speak code, we are always busy decoding one another's conversation, which deeply influences the way we relate to each other. If the scene is eluding you, write the subtext for the other character as well as your own, and see if it isn't wonderfully clarifying.

THE ARC

This is the difference between what your character wants and feels at the beginning and at the end. There's arc for the whole play, the act, the scene, and even the beat. Pick a section you are working on and think about it. Once you can articulate a starting and finishing point, look for the fulcrum moment where your character starts the journey away from A and begins the transformation to B. Yes, you can go on a journey from Peoria to Peoria, but who wants to? And more important, who wants to see it? What really animates a major character is change. The arc helps define what that change is. When working on the play as a whole, it is valuable to start with the end, define it, and then go back to the beginning and make sure it is situated differently. Remember that the arc can also be used on microsections for spot work. Arcs also enforce variety and give you the crucial sense of the role as a whole. Without it, you can get lost in the details.

BACKSTORY

This is the character's offstage history, both mentioned in the text and imagined by the actor. Backstory helps you explain behavior, stimulates you emotionally, and allows you to deepen and make more dramatic key moments and scenes. Don't develop the backstory until your character understanding is quite advanced. Use backstory to assist in clarifying your behavior. If you can't point to the line in the play that your backstory affects in a way that helps you make a point the playwright wants to make, don't go to the trouble. The wrong backstory produces the wrong moment. The childhood you imagine must produce the character the playwright imagines. Backstory is not playwriting; it is supportive evidence for the case the text makes. Don't play the character to support your backstory. Create the backstory to heighten circumstances clearly in the play—best done after a week of studying text and revised in rehearsal.

THEME THREADS

If you don't know what the play's about, how are you going to recognize the important moments? If you don't recognize the important moments, how are you going to act the part? Don't neglect the big picture. Theme threads are strings of meaning that run through the play. This is about loneliness, that's about loneliness, over here they mention loneliness. Hmmm, could be a theme thread. When you've identified five or six theme threads in the text and subtext, write them in order and see if you can think of a category that includes all or most of them. This is a central theme. Now take the theme to the text and identify moments that explicate the theme or theme threads. These are likely to be important moments—important to give focus to and play interestingly and well. The basic idea is that without a map of the big picture, it's difficult to make the little things work. You owe several hours to this process.

TECHNIQUE

CLAIMING THE SPACE

There are mysteries in acting, and this is one of them. Why is it that some actors and some performances do what we call "hold stage"? I personally think it's an absence of fear. When shards or splinters of your fear of the role, the play, and your adequacy are present ("I shouldn't really be up here, I know you're not going to be interested in me"), the audience senses that desperate edge and retreats from it. The actor's physical and emotional discomfort makes the audience uncomfortable as well. The actor who truly feels the right to be in the space claims the space. This right is based on pursuing simple, completeable tasks that result in the character fulfilling her needs. Do that, and you'll feel this complex of fears recede. Fail to do it, and you'll sweat. Oh, and make friends with the space, which is the frame for your endeavors. Come early and take it in visually and orally. Move through it. Feel the space by becoming part of its architecture. Sense it through your feet and your body. Become a comfortable part of its volume. Now pursue your character's task and the stage is yours.

BALANCE

For reasons mysterious even to me, I was an amateur boxer for ten years. For my trouble, my nose was broken six times, but it did result in the following advice to the actor: Onstage seek a balance point for the body that will allow you to move quickly and decisively in any direction at any moment. The boxer is poised to throw a punch from any angle. The actor is poised to respond. Now to achieve this physical readiness, the boxer's feet are sixteen to twenty inches apart, but acting doesn't always allow that. It is the *sense* of this balance that is crucial. Your body should tell you that it could move right, left, backward, or forward without further adjustment. A marvelous thing about this sense of prepared balance is that it almost immediately deepens your concentration and drags you into the present moment, a state of being that any actor covets. When possible, the knees should be unlocked and the body relaxed but poised. We are then ready to respond to impulse and give it physical form. One of the nicest things for the actor is that it gives increased physical capacity without the broken nose.

HANDS OVER YOUR HEAD!

If I had, God help me, filmed all the acting classes I've taught and reviewed them, I think I would find that less than 1 percent of these young actors ever had their hands above their shoulders or below their knees. You're probably thinking I have finally gone over the edge, but we're talking about virgin gestural territory here. What this tells me is that culturally we absorb the information that nice people don't do such things, and whatever you're not supposed to do provides rich exploration for the actor. Almost every large part, and many small ones, embodies moments of wild feeling, desperate circumstances, or comic explosiveness. When those moments come, you may find a use for these places the hands and arms never go. What I suggest here is that you need to give your body permission to explore the wilder shores of its possibilities. Otherwise, you will be unwittingly trapped in the Miss Manners' school of socially acceptable gesture.

BREATHE

When you need to get into the moment, when you need to be really present for the other actors, when you need to actually think onstage—breathe. Forgetting to breathe has been shown by several studies to be a primary component of panic. And panic, need I say, is not helpful to the acting process. Breathing centers you, calms you, promotes attention and concentration, and prevents your nerves from turning you into a whirling dervish. I have a friend who says he is so beset by adrenaline onstage that he writes the word *breathe* between the thumb and forefinger of his left hand to remind himself while he's acting. When you're not breathing, you are entirely focused on yourself. You need regular breath to liberate you to be *with* the other actors. I'm not kidding. Make breathing a priority in your next rehearsal or performance, and notice the change in your work. For one thing you'll be less afraid of silence and the pause, because your breathing fills it.

THE MEANINGFUL OBJECT

A prop remains just a prop until it becomes a vehicle for your character's hopes, dreams, rage, and joy. Let's have that object in the play—the one you kiss in victory or throw against the wall in defeat. Finding the props that do these things for you and the play heightens and expands your performance; otherwise, it's all just dishware. Which object in this play reminds you of your greatest loss? Which makes you the saddest? What object would your character carry first from a burning house or most miss after a robbery? These props are characters for you and with them you have powerful relationships. These props ground you and make the moments. Do you have these props in the play you're doing? Is there something specific you need? Don't be afraid to ask. On the other hand, some props are useful to the character because they are absent. You always look for a certain toy in your childhood room, but it's long gone. Make your character's relationship to the play's things as rich as his relationship to the people. Give those things personal histories. Befriend them.

THE ENERGY-DEPRIVING OBSTACLE

Let's recap. The action is what you want the other person to do, to feel, or to understand. The obstacles are what prevent your from easily completing the action. Now, sometimes the obstacle depletes the action's energy. For instance, the obstacle forces you to talk very quietly (the bad guy is only ten feet away), and this seems to suck the energy out of the scene. You can restore the dramatic drive by increasing the urgency. What you say is quiet, yes, but the need in your void is powerful and palpable, which keeps the text theatrical. Urgency is most easily applied as a reaction to time pressure. You must achieve the action in five minutes or die the death of ten thousand cuts. When the obstacle seems to make the scene founder, become placid, flaccid, or passive, look for a circumstance that demands urgency and then redouble yours.

VOCAL ENERGY

All right folks, the scene may not be playing because the vocal energy is too low. Everything else is co-pacetic. The action is clear; the obstacle is established. You're concentrating. The problem is that the lack of vocal energy is sapping the rest of your energy. This is where the very old-fashioned and somehow tackily British "speak up" can work wonders. To speak up takes an increase of energy. That increase, almost by itself, seems to heighten the stakes of what is currently playing. At the same time, this new energy radiates to all parts of the body and you feel impulses to move and *do*. The new drive to *do* naturally focuses you on "do what" and "how come"—thus refocusing you on the action. This forces the other actor to relate, and in a trice, everything's getting better simply because you spoke up. Its other virtue is that, to start with, it's not complicated emotionally or physically to do what's requested. Last step! Don't wait for others; request it of yourself.

THE PERFORMANCE DANGER OF THE SMALL LAUGH

All goes well. You've got a succulent role in a delightful comedy and even your mother loves it. What could go wrong now that you've opened? Well for one thing, you could go hunting for the small laugh. There is a point in comedy where enough is enough. You're telling the story, you're getting some laughs, so don't succumb to laugh fever. It starts this way: There are three or four places where perhaps nine or ten people are chuckling, and it occurs to you that by broadening your playing or by being twice as cute or twice as loud you could build that orphan into a big-time roar. First, you probably can't because the script's situation doesn't support it. Second, by inflating that moment you may be distorting the scene's natural rhythm and/or stealing focus from a more important character touch that follows. Once you're open, keep your hunger for hilarity in the cage. Remember that laughter is usually a by-product of story and circumstance. They aren't gunfighter notches. Leave well enough alone.

FINISHING

We can improve our acting by knowing and showing when something is over. Let's start with the punctuation, specifically the period. Yes, there are such
moments as blending two sentences, but usually we
need to bring something to a halt at the period. This
also implies that we start something new with the
next sentence. We have to *hear* the finish and recognize the new start. Beyond the period, there's another world of endings. There's the moment when
you've made your point or listened as long as you
can stand it. There's the time when there's no use
continuing as before. The instant when you demand
a change of subject, you need to be aware of the finish and act it. In life when the meeting's over, we
often rise to signify it. Signaling to the audience
when something is over is part of your job. Finishing is often important to the character as a sign of
power or control. Be decisive. Provide closure. To
stop is an active choice. Stop.

ILLUSTRATION

Be careful not to illustrate the line. If for instance the speech is "I saw the big cat crouch and then spring forward, loping across the scrub brush toward the tall pines," it's probably not necessary for you to literally crouch, spring, and lope, or describe with gesture the difference between a tall and a short pine. The audience understood all that from the language. Acting it out would be, as one of my favorite character actors used to say, "too much of a muchness." There are, of course, moments when the actor glares balefully while he speaks of a baleful glare, but not, let us hope, too damned often. This illustrated form of acting lacks mystery and psychology. Remember that the tension between what the actor thinks and what she says is crucial. Illustration innately talks down to the audience creating the embarrassing sense that if you didn't act a muskrat when you said "muskrat," they just wouldn't get it. Have mercy!

PAPER TOWELS

Actors are continually running out of things to do: "I drank the coffee and put the cup in the sink, now what can I do?" Well, break what's available down into its component parts (remember we spend weeks without the real props). Let's say you spill spaghetti sauce on the floor and you want to clean it up.

1. Look for and get the roll of paper towels.
2. Take it out of the wrapper.
3. Open the door to the garbage.
4. Throw the wrapper in the garbage.
5. Rip off two sets of three towels each.
6. Put one set on the table.
7. Get down and wipe up the spaghetti sauce.
8. Throw first towels in the garbage.
9. Further clean with second set of towels.
10. Throw away.
11. Put the roll back in the cabinet.
12. Sit down.

And this is all done while talking. See, there was plenty to do. You just hadn't broken it down.

GOING BUT NOT KNOWING

OK, everybody knows (and everybody says) the great trick is to perform as if you didn't know what was going to happen next. Simple enough, but you do know. So, how to proceed. Look at it this way: You've got to work on the problems of the present and stay out of the future. You have a current goal (the action). She says a line. Does what she say get you closer or put you further away from what you're trying to achieve? React to the positive or negative nature of her lines. It is your current reaction based only on current information that keeps you in the moment. If you're still projecting, try slowing down. If you give yourself time to perceive the present, you are more likely to act in it. Also, check to see if right this instant (not at the end of the scene), you have something to lose. The current danger keeps you current. You stay in the present by pursuing the present need, even if it's not as dramatic as the crisis ten pages on. It's when the present moment doesn't seem to have interesting acting possibilities that you tend to play the future—which, remember, only the tarot cards know.

STANDARD AMERICAN PACE

And now the sort of heretical statement that can get you burned at the theatrical stake. I believe there is such a thing as Standard American Pace, and if we were aware of it and used it as a benchmark to depart from, we could solve a good many rehearsal problems straight away. Here's the deal: Standard American Pace consists of the following: line, one beat, line, one beat, line, one beat. The demand of this format generates an immediately sufficient stage energy. Using this as a basis, you vary it rhythmically as the psychology and complexity demands. When the text and the actor are in full cry, you pick up the cue directly off the last word. Need more time for thought, take two beats. Anything above two beats right on up to an endless fifteen is used to make points. Put it this way, if you don't have something important to do with the silence, you don't get more than two beats. Let's call this a workable oversimplification. It's how most American productions work and how their rhythms deliver content.

DETAILS: THE HEART OF ACTING

A man enters a room; he automatically reaches for the light switch he knows is there. He goes to the refrigerator, opens it, takes out a beer, then puts it back. He closes the refrigerator door and idly wipes a smudge off the handle. He smiles thinking how often his wife has asked him to do that. He remembers to take off his shoes because they are muddy, and then puts the ends of the laces inside because it's neater. These are acting details. There would be details of a different sort if he were speaking: interesting turns in the thought process, surprising emphasis, a clear understanding of who he was talking to and for what purpose. The telling details of thought and action are the difference between the good actor and the average actor. As they say, the devil is in the details, but developing details that reveal the character and the script is hard, laborious, careful work. Do it or be damned.

CONFIDENT ACTOR: HANDS AT SIDES

Ah yes, sometimes a good acting idea becomes so prevalent in American theater training that it lives on to become an unbearable cliché. In the sixties, with realism in the saddle and all forms of behavior transmogrified into eccentric physical tics, we all longed for actors who stood still, commanded the stage, kept their hands at their sides, and made their points without being fussy. Well, careful what you wish for. We got them—now our stages are littered with steely-eyed, confident actors commanding the stage without moving a muscle. It's sort of like Madame Tussaud's. Remember, there are moments that electrify because of their tense, coiled stillness, but most of the time we're brushing taco chips off our pants, going through our pockets for our keys, cleaning our glasses, or tapping out songs on our chests. You have to be careful that standing still with your hands at your sides doesn't read as being petrified of acting and not knowing what to do with yourself.

ARTICULATION

American voice teachers' techniques and applications have become increasingly sophisticated, but down in the actors' trenches, the simplest thing of all is still a problem. Articulation. It almost seems that the actor is taught so many things to concentrate on—from actions, to obstacles, to circumstances, to philosophies of space, to spinal alignment—that he often forgets to move his lips and deliver the words as if their arrival in the audience's ear were crucial. Let me say this twice for emphasis. The actor's major responsibility is to deliver the text. Once more, the actor's major responsibility is to deliver the text. Nothing else the actor does can compensate for failing this responsibility. And text delivery primarily depends on the consonants. Bite them, explode them, concentrate on them until it becomes second nature. Physical theater may be on the rise, but the text retains its primacy. Articulation.

OVERUSE

Actors do a hundred things, but they usually have one or two things that have been winners in the past that they do ad infinitum. What's your version? This actor who cries easily, cries all the time. This actor who gets laughs when he laughs, laughs a dozen times in every production. This actor (male and female) fetchingly shakes her golden curls. That actor slaps his thigh for emphasis. (Who have you ever seen slap his thigh in real life?) This actor invariably climbs up on the furniture. That actor endlessly chops the air in the same way for emphasis. These sometimes shrewdly habitual patterns can be useful if you change cities with every production, but in most cases, the audience is beginning to recognize them as belonging to the actor not the text or psychology. Often, as in selective forgetting, the actor doesn't know she's doing it. Sometimes the actor does it because he knows the audience will laugh or gasp (Olivier showed nothing but the whites of his eyes in several productions). Careful, they're on to you.

ATTACKING THE LINE

There are moments when we go from silence to speech that take care of themselves. These are usually moments when the story is carrying us, when the situation is so intense or so surprising that the audience leans forward to catch the slightest whisper. These aren't the majority of moments, however. Most of the time the actor has to attack the top of the line, enlivening it with a dollop of extra energy. Why? First, you need to take back the focus after the other actor speaks. Second, if what the other actor says doesn't energize you, why should it engage the audience? Some actors become death-ray energy drains, always sliding into their line under the level of the line before. There needs to be a steadily reinvigorated vocal energy to keep the text aloft and functioning. Acting is, by definition, not passive work, and most actors in most situations must demand our attention with the first three or four words of the sentence. Attack!

FINISH THE BROKEN LINE

"So James," I say, "when the character says, 'Listen, I . . .' what's the rest of the line?" James stares at me sullenly and replies coolly, "He cuts me off at that point." "Yes, James, we know that, but if he didn't cut you off, what would you have said?" The silence is long. The reason you must know what the cut line is, is that otherwise it will be clear as day to both the audience and the other actor that you're faking it (truly, it's one of the most obvious frauds in acting). This fraud breaks everyone's sense of belief not only in your work but in the story. *Continue the cut line* until the other actor interrupts you. If he hasn't been interrupting you, your keeping trucking will instruct him. If the other actor has difficulty cutting you, give him a split second at the end of the written section while you "think." This allows you a sense of continuance and gives him a small window to pick up the text.

UPSTAGED

Ah, a nostalgic tip! Nobody talks about being up-staged anymore. It's become the stage crime that dare not speak its name. Just for the record, when you're acting on a proscenium stage (they still exist, drat their horizontal little natures) and the other actor is constantly anywhere from a step to a league closer to the set than you are, it forces you to turn up to play with her and the audience can't see your face. These days the crime is committed more sub-tly than in the past. Last week I watched a two-character play, and one actor was invariably six inches upstage of the other all night long. What to do when you're locked in battle with one of these stage thieves? Simple. Turn front. If necessary, turn front and move downstage. Play with the other actor verbally—but face the audience. You'll get the focus you need, and that bad girl (or boy) will shortly have to move down on your level to make contact with you. Do this enough, and the other actor will get the idea and share.

WHEN TO KNOW THE LINES

Everybody has their druthers. The majority of actors I've worked with say they don't learn the lines
until a scene is blocked because their memory
works better in association with the physical moves.
As a director, I can't help feeling irritated by people
who hold the book too long. There's an awkward
period when the actor puts down the script but isn't
really secure. It's a moderately wasted time for the
director, and I live to get it over with as soon as possible. Here's what I would do. After the second rehearsal, ask the director clearly when she wants the
lines learned. Very often this is left open-ended, but
the director, believe me, has an unspoken agenda.
Oh, and one other thing, if you have one of the
smaller roles be off-book *before* the actors with
heavier line loads. Actors who don't are noted by
the director and usually not rehired. My personal
view is that the actor should be off-book the next
time he works on a scene that has been blocked.

THOUGHTS PER MINUTE

The actor of genius registers more thoughts per minute than the good actor, who registers more thoughts per minute than the average actor, who registers way more thoughts per minute than the bad actor, who registers practically no thoughts per minute. The firelight quality of the mind onstage endlessly fascinates us. The character's active mind takes in information, processes information, and gives out information, and the way it moves from one to the other rivets us. For the character's mind to do this, you need to be steeped in the circumstances, applying an action, using tactics to achieve it, and being aware of what you're getting from the other actor based on the history and complexity of the relationship. Far too often the actor moves too little emotional and circumstantial information through the playing, and thus the audience has nothing to do but wait for the special effects. Your brain is the most theatrical event onstage.

LOVE SCENES

Love onstage is, in the main, the lover's action of wanting the best for the other person in the given circumstances. Secondarily, it demands a focus on removing the obstacles that are preventing love's fruition. It is not the infuriating saccharine tone used to signal, in capitals, THE LOVE SCENE. Is there a desire for touch, a drive toward sexuality? Obviously, that should be a result of the above, not its primary focus. Remember the movies where you waited ninety minutes for the kiss? The audience, sensing the chemistry, roots for the solution to removing the obstacle, and it is on the obstacle that you, the actor, should keep your focus. The other quality crucial to *amore* onstage is appreciation of the other's qualities. Don't just love, love something she *does*. Do *not* endlessly signal the audience that you are romantically and sexually available. This usually results in behavior so bizarre the audience looks away in embarrassment. Now go ahead, love!

BRING THE BODY, DON'T ADD IT

If you watch, with great interest, actors and acting for a very long time, you can't help categorizing. There exists a large group of actors who during what one might call the "figuring out stage" of rehearsal, lasting up to two weeks, put their bodies on hold. The impulses that would otherwise animate them physically seem derailed or devoted entirely to their thoughts, their examinations. During this period, one might think they have directed their nervous systems to carry *no* impulses rather than risk the wrong ones. They cogitate like wax columns. Nothing moves. Later they warm up and begin to allow their bodies into the act, but they have already lost the opportunity to try it a dozen different ways. From the very beginning, allow any impulses you have to provide a physicality. A thought occurs to you, let it reach your torso, feet, and hands. It's never too early, and you can constantly revise and change. Bring that body!

THE TWO MINDS OF THE ACTOR

Great acting usually works on two contradictory levels simultaneously. On the one hand, we are *in* the role; we become the character in the situation. Using ourselves (but submerging ourselves), we play as if the situation is real. A second self, however, simultaneously calculates acting possibilities, "If she's doing that, then I have to change what I'm doing." "Wow, that's the first time I really ever heard that line. It's much more hostile than I imagined. I can't go on being affectionate." "I've been in this chair for three pages, when can I move?" This second self is always seeking acting possibilities and looks and listens for them. You pay attention to the other actor both within the confines of your character and as an actor saying, "Well, if he does that, I would have to do this." The actor is aware both of her belief in the situation and of the acting opportunities that are presented. This dual awareness is useful because we often become self-regarding as we inhabit character, and that second level helps us look outward.

CROCODILE TEARS

First of all, are tears truly necessary to the moment? Most of the time in life we strive mightily not to cry. Won't that suffice? All right, for some unknown reason, these tears are crucial to the moment. We want the tears, naturally, coming out of your involvement in the circumstances or your substitution of an event in your life. But hey, nobody's perfect, and it's just not happening. What now? (Now this is going to get us both in trouble, so pretend it's not in the book.) My mother used to say that she would always rub her eyes a minute before the moment and then contrive to look into the lights. "Always worked," she said. My father more elaborately Scotch taped a small sliver of onion along the inside of the second joint of his index finger. "I'd put my hand over my eyes for a second, boom, always worked like a charm." My daughter Jessica says her acting generation relies on Tiger Balm, a smidgen between the fingers and then transferred to the eyes. Careful, though, that stuff is powerful! (And don't mention I told you.)

VOICE CONSCIOUS

I always remember my actress mother's disapproving look when she would say, "He's one of those actors who listens to his own voice." You can recognize these performers, right? God willing, you're not one of them. They, like Narcissus, have fallen in love with their own tonalities and are often gardening their own pitch and resonance rather than playing the scene with you. These poor souls were probably overcomplimented by family and friends on their "lovely" voice, and now, sonorous as all get out, they are driving us mad. Concentrate on the action and stop listening to yourself! If you have a good voice, you are blessed, but be careful not to lean on it as a substitute for other acting virtues. When being chased by a tiger, you won't be concentrating on your basso profundo. In acting, you're always chasing the tiger or being chased. Deal with that and leave your voice alone.

PUNCTUATING WITH REACTIONS

Don't be an actor who shuts down his systems while someone else does a big speech. The other's big speech is there to have an impact on you, and minus that impact, the speech will seem marooned—the traditional voice crying in the wilderness. Not only do we need to see the impact of the speech on you, your reactions are crucial to the transitions in that speech. So, in the midst of this backyard oration, she says, "So I don't care what you think. This might have been your business ten years ago." By allowing your reaction to fall after the word *think*, where the period punctuates the moment, you create the transition needed so the actor speaking can move forward. The audience doesn't simply focus like a laser on the speaker. They *look* for the reaction. Think of yourself as assisting the punctuation of the big speech, even when it isn't yours. There are no monologues when others are onstage. The listener creates the duologue.

DO IT ANOTHER WAY

You're locked in. The part's nailed down. In a sense, you're doing it like a checklist. I do this, then I do this, and finally, this. It's safe. You feel confident and in control, but the flip side is a certain hollowness, a mechanical tinge. You know what the action is, what the circumstances are. Trust yourself. Play a little. Keep the structure; change the moments. Kill that wonderful gesture you've built into the moment a dozen times in a row. Let go of that reading that's become pickled. Sit a line later. Add a new prop. Handle the phone differently. If the section is repeated three times, change the details of what you're doing three times. Often, a small change or two lures your creativity back from exile. Sometimes it's astounding: You change a locked-in gesture, and suddenly you feel alive and flooded with new ideas. The difference between focussing your concentration on finding a new way versus repeating your delivery is often the difference between fresh and stale. Unshackle yourself. You'll both survive and prosper!

PAYING OFF THE PROP

Think of the prop as a baby. Once one comes into your life, you can't just leave it on a doorstep. The prop probably has an original purpose that is quite clear. When Meg (in *Crimes of the Heart*) asks Lennie if she knows the best lawyer in town to represent their sister Babe, she might drag out the local phone directory to look up "lawyers." The prop has now been introduced, but we can't simply abandon it. How can the phone book be paid off in a way that furthers story, character, or relationship? Well, Lennie has stayed home in their small hometown taking on the family responsibilities, while Meg has gone off in search of fame and fortune. Now Meg is back intimating Lennie can't handle things. In the midst of their argument, Lennie might rip the phone book (her phone book, by the way) out of Meg's hands and slam it back in the drawer, regaining the initiative. The prop (the phone book) has been *both* introduced and paid off.

SECONDARY FOCUS

I was watching a Beth Henley play last week, and in one of her wonderful monologues, the actor stared across the table at her scene partner unrelievedly throughout. First, it denied any physicality. Second, for audience members seated house right, it meant they saw her profile (at best). Always find a reason to give your focus (and your unparalleled beauty) to all parts of the house. All right, you're seated at a table center, playing across to your partner. Changing the focus to out front is easy. You've doubtless noticed that when people have to think about something while they are talking, they often look away from you and look back when they know what they want to say to you. Good, that takes care of looking center. Now, you need to contrive a reason to look left (away from your partner at the table). Is the coffee on and you have to check it? Are you expecting a pizza delivery and did you just hear something? Find reasons to cover the stage with your focus.

TRYING THE TOP

We, being the conservative, guarded creatures we are, usually respond to what happens to us onstage in a very middling way. After all, it would be tasteless if we did "too much," eh? Let's break that pattern and see what happens if we go big. When your sister confides in you that she has shot her husband, don't simply cast a distracted glance at the ceiling, literally fall backward out of your chair onto the floor or swallow that rose you've been sniffing. Director gives you the thumbs down? Fine, small is always available. But remember, something ballsier, something wild and even absurd, may carry the day and take you to a new level. A word to the wise: I would wait to experiment until the middle of the rehearsal period when you're beginning to feel knowledgeable about the role. Then look at several key moments in the text that are connected to the play's emotional center and risk a larger, more extreme response. When you hit it wrong, you just size it back down. When you hit it right, it's astounding. Get out of the middle a little. You have nothing to lose.

GETTING TO THE GOOD PART

I was watching a performance the other night and I thought, "Oh dear, this poor fool thinks it's *all* the good part. Where's the part he simply has to get through to *get* to the good part?" You know how that goes. Here you are giving directions to your directionally challenged spouse. He knows how to get to the library, so you tell him that part quickly, without emphasis, rushing through it, and then slow down and emphasize the tricky part going over the bridge. Where, dear actor, is the part you rush through to get to the good part? If you don't rush through any of it, how will we know what *is* the good part? Actors tend to treat every sentence as if it was precious plutonium. Find the dross and treat it like dross so the gold will shine. Find the part of the text you can rush through so quickly that it's right on the edge of being impenetrable. These are the parts where you say, "I know you already know this, and it's so simple I'm almost embarrassed to be saying it, but you see it leads me to . . ." Go ahead, rush.

TECHNIQUE AND CONTENT

Know what the content is then use your technique to reveal it. Technique, for instance, may be your trained sense of cutting away what isn't needed, of using a stillness as counterpoint to profound emotion. The stillness, however, is of no use if you don't know what the moments are that shatter it, explode it. Stillness is the negative space allowing strong line and bright color full impact. The explosions are there to reveal content, so is the stillness. Technique cannot reveal to us which goes where. I often see technique obliterate content in performance. Technique is "how"; content is "what." Remember that we must define "what" before we can apply "how." Technique can allow us to cover an emotional moment we can't reach, or provide the fireworks that reveal a key plot point, but it *cannot tell the story*. Do your homework, my technique-heavy friends. Don't go throwing its weight around at the expense of content. It can be embarrassing.

THE GIRL WITH THE FIXATED EYES

There they are, unavoidable, those eyes that never leave yours. You act, and they bore into you. My God, they don't even blink? Some actors seem to believe that eye contact is meant to be as eternal as death and taxes. It can drive you so crazy you're afraid to look at them. Simple as this seems, let's talk about it for a minute. Humans don't make constant eye contact (well maybe when they're trying to be seductive). Our eyes move away and then back, or on rare occasions, avoid consistently. Remember that *where* and *when* you look can be both character- and plot-defining. Your job is not simply the other actor's eyes. Looking away often provides the obstacle in the scene. Often it provokes blocking as in: I move around to the other side of the sofa in search of your eyes. Remember that withholding your eyes is as powerful as giving them. The moment you give after withholding can be powerful. Don't be the lock-eyed monster.

PLAYING ARENA

No, you don't have to spin like a lazy Susan. However . . .

1. The principles of acting are all the same, you just have to find reasons to be seen by everyone.
2. When you look away from the other actor, simply find a point of concentration that allows people behind you to see you in profile.
3. Some reactions have to be carried all the way round in a circle.
4. People don't mind not seeing your face for a couple of minutes. After that, a slight adjustment of your chair or a piece of blocking can solve the problem.
5. It's your job, too, not just the director's.
6. Find circumstances that allow you to be more diverse in the space. Is Godzilla coming? Look behind you.
7. In comedy, you often need to "pan" your reaction to the laugh line. The best way is to justify a move on the reaction.

Mainly, simply stay aware of long sequences in one position. Duh.

THE STRAIGHT MAN

We all want to play the funniest or most emotional role, but who is setting up the belly laugh or the emotional breakdown? What if we're cast in that role? The straight man used to be an honored profession for both men and women. It is the theatrical equivalent of the person in volleyball who sets so the other person can spike. These parts, the straight parts, offer wonderful opportunities for careful analysis and complex playing. How, in comedy, should the laugh line be set up? Do you need to be aggressive and loud, so the joke can be delivered quietly and offhandedly? Or should it be the reverse? Should you be sitting or standing? Should you feed the line quickly or slowly? How should you react after the comic line to build the laugh? In drama, how precisely do you need to prepare the atmosphere for Lear's madness? What is your responsibility in fueling Medea's rage? The great roles remain dependent on first-rate work by the straight man. Remember, you are there to provide what's needed. What's needed?

WHO YOU TALKING TO, HAMLET?

Yes, the soliloquy needs context. The director, irritated with your constant questions, says testily, "You're talking to the audience." As if that solves the problem. Who comprises the audience? Are they the King's court? Are they all psychiatrists? Are they assumed to be friends or enemies? If they are simply "the audience" in all their divergent splendor, then what is it your character wants from them? I have heard reputable directors of Shakespeare brush off such questions by saying, "It was simply a device in Elizabethan theater." Yeah? And how does that help? Don't forget the simple maxim that you need to be talking for a specific reason in a specific context. Just "talking" isn't a solution and leaves the speech in limbo with declined impact. If you have a series of soliloquies or monologues directed to the audience, perhaps you could change their nature each time. This one I'm saying to fathers everywhere, and this one is definitely to Poseidon. Give these speeches a logic beyond simple presentation.

SETTING THE READING

You practiced the line at home and now you're doing it exactly like that in rehearsal. Why not? Because the actor whose mind is engaged in remembering a predecided reading is not present and reacting in the moment. This actor is not reactive; she is simply engaged in a mechanical act of isolation. Acting is not a memory trick; it is alive in the moment. You want to know the meaning of the line and the circumstances in which it is formulated. You want to know the action it carries forward and the obstacles it faces. You want to take into account what the other actor is giving and doing. Out of all these considerations, emphasis is born. If you are hopelessly, irremediably addicted to setting emphasis, try slowly weaning yourself by choosing three readings and picking between them on your feet. At least you'll be thinking in the moment. Emphasis set in concrete is usually a recipe for second-rate acting. Trust yourself not to decide until the moment.

RELISH

Relish means to take keen or zestful pleasure. Zestful pleasure! Where's that in what you're feeling, Mr. Oedipus? After your best performances, audience members often say to you, "You really seemed to be having a good time!" In drama, they tend to remark on your intensity and profound belief in the situation. In comedy, they usually mean you played the absurdity of the situation with fanatic sincerity. The audience sees "relish" as the actor's pleasure in concentration and situation. It sees "zest" as the energy applied to the play's problems and story. It sees "pleasure" as the actor taking on the demands of the role as if there were nothing—*nothing*—she would rather be doing. See that actor playing for high stakes? Now that's relish! Yes, there are characters who have lost their zest, but when they carry a heavy load in the production, what sustains their energy? When people in tough situations are described as fighters, we identify with their zest for battle, their relish for the din and clangor. Find the character's relish; it's an audience favorite.

OVERPAUSED

When you read the memoirs of the leading actors and directors of the theatrical generation holding sway between 1930 and 1960, they seem almost invariably miffed by the "younger generation" taking too many "pauses." Taking the inevitable generational warfare with a grain of salt, it's still worth considering (in actor training I find they take too few). The pause mainly falls into three categories: thinking, emphasis, and emotional blockage. Thinking pauses are usually brief; the emotional pause where feelings prevent speech occurs at key moments only. It's that pause for emphasis that can be overused. Let's say the line is: "Well, I know you're worried about your brother and there was a little accident, but he's all right. It's Louise who's hurt." You see immediately you could take at least four pauses for emphasis. Perhaps you should take only one. You choose where. It obviously depends on which piece of information is the key plot point, the most dramatic, the most psychologically crucial. The thirties generation knew endless pauses for emphasis made the speech incomprehensible. Remember, emphasis is strategic as well as intuitive.

THE DOUBLE TAKE

All right, I know you've been waiting for this, what precisely is a double take and how would I use it in *Hamlet*? Most of us think the double take exited with vaudeville, but here's what it's about—surprise and recognition. The double take is the sudden understanding that the situation just got extremely interesting. That means it's potentially a tool for *Oedipus* as well as *A Funny Thing Happened on the Way to the Forum*. The mechanics are these: Something intrudes on your attention while you're doing or thinking about something else. You assume it's less interesting than what you're doing, so you throw it a quick cursory glance and look back at your own work. Suddenly you realize the possible implications of what you've just seen and refocus on it with your full attention. If it's Groucho Marx leading a rhinoceros, it's comedy. If it's Hamlet realizing the slight movement behind the arras is Polonius, it's drama. Mechanics: Glance left (or right) quickly and look back to the original point; now look left again with sudden or full attention. Bingo. They'll be doing them in the first regional theater on Mars.

THE SCALD AND THE BANDAGE

I used to work in a pre-Starbucks coffeeshop where the job demanded doing about three things at once. The net result was that I spilled boiling water on myself about once a day. Let's call that "the scald." As soon as I did it, I reached for the ice and applied it. That's obviously the "bandage." Look for those moments where something somebody else says or does metaphorically scalds you. Let yourself react as instantaneously and painfully as if you had been burned. Don't hold back the reaction and don't underplay it. Treat those words exactly as if they burned you. (Obviously we don't do this six times in the same play.) If the play and character is decently written, the next thing that character will do is apply some kind of bandage to the wound. Just thinking of the next speech (sometimes it's allowing yourself to get angry) as a bandage allows you to better understand the subtext. Find the scald, understand the bandage.

FRAMING THE IDEA

Speech is an idea made audible. The idea onstage may take the form of a declaration, a question, a suggestion, a defense, a reversal, and so on. The acting question, of course, is whether the idea has already been conceived and the speech is the result, or whether the idea hits literally the moment before and the speech is a first try at articulation. In other words, are you having an idea or developing an idea? Depending on your choice, the speech has a very different shape and feeling. The actor makes this choice over and over in the role. Such choices are constant and the result deeply defining. The choice is sometimes a result of study and sometimes intuitive and spontaneous. What isn't often understood is that the result of these choices is, in fact, a characterization, an outline of how this particular person gets and handles her ideas. I guess I'm saying you need to have an idea about the form of the ideas.

A RHYTHM THING

The focus goes where the rhythm changes. If you've been speaking quickly and suddenly speak slowly, the audience takes in this new "slow" with particular attention and interest. The same is true with a new "fast," "loud," or "soft." Remember that once a rhythm establishes itself, we are lulled by it, only to be startled awake when it changes. Naturally, this is only helpful when the point of change is important to narrative or character. Take a football offense. You establish the run to score with the pass. Rhythm creates a tension because the audience realizes it will be broken somewhere in some way, and it waits to see how. If you're loud for a while, you will make a big point with silence. Think about those moments you really want the audience to get, and then figure out how you might change the rhythm at that point. You can use rhythm to give focus. The real question is, focus to what?

THE LIFT

Alas, acting energy often runs downhill. The scene or speech starts with a burst but slowly settles into a lower metabolic rate. Sometimes the actors pick up this passive level from each other. Every once in a while we need to reset the energy at a higher level. That moment of reenergizing the scene I'll call "the lift." Now please remember this isn't a ploy to maintain manic energy. Enough manic energy, we all know, is more than enough. This is a recognition that at various times we need to reinvest in our commitment to push the acting out into the house. The time to lift is usually at the point of the new idea. Having finished one thing, we need to introduce the next with a little panache. Each actor monitors the scene to make sure it is being played at a level that engages the audience's attention. When it isn't, someone (you) must take the responsibility and lift.

PRONOUNS

All right, I seem to be in the minority here, but I wish to confront the developing cabal against emphasizing pronouns. I've never met any of the people who teach this dogma, but I vote for a full reappraisal. It started out as common wisdom for speaking Shakespeare: "Don't hit the pronoun; the pronoun is defined by the sentence." But now it's leaking over into plays of all sorts, and that makes it downright dangerous. Sometimes we need to hit the pronoun to clarify a difference as in, "It's not Julie. *He's* the one I'm talking about." Sometimes we need to hit the pronoun so we know what the speaker thinks of this person. How you say *he* in "he drives me crazy" helps me understand your attitude toward this particular person. Here's my rule: Hit the pronoun when it assists clarity or characterization. Yes, even in Shakespeare. And down with the cabal.

THE OPENING-NIGHT
SYNDROME

I went to my opening last night, and the amphetamine pusher who haunts openings had really done a job! The actors had decided that if the play had been good before, it was *really* going to be good for press and parents. The actors played at energy levels unimagined during rehearsals. They threw themselves at the play like diving birds at a window. It was infinitely louder and infinitely faster, accompanied by wild gesticulation, and general mayhem was employed by all. Gone were the rests and pauses, and all rhythm disappeared in the general blur. I sat horrified. Who were these demons? They were actors "doing it *better.*" Moral: Play the show you had in rehearsal. Don't psyche yourself up to give one all-or-nothing performance. As a matter of fact, calm yourself down for the opening. Soothing tea, sounds of the ocean, books on Zen. Just say no to adrenaline. Please.

PLAYING DUMB

The character who doesn't get it is a comic tradition, a tragic flaw, and a dramatic obstacle. When you're cast in this way, how do you create limited understanding from the inside? Now, we all have a hard time absorbing certain kinds of information that others master easily. When it comes to computers and mathematics, I'm definitely dim. The key is simply treating what you are confronted with as extremely complicated. Treat directions to a nearby market as plans for a nuclear device. Don't play "I can't understand." Play "I'm striving to understand." A second technique is to place your concentration off the point. My thirteen-year-old daughter may not absorb the simplest requests while she is watching television. Add large sums in your head while others speak to you. The third possibility is that the character actively doesn't want to know or understand. She doesn't like or respect the information being given. Or, lastly, play that you don't speak the language. Remember, you still need to play an action. In this case, you may choose an action off the point. By misdirecting your action, you will have played dumb.

DIALECTS FREEDOM

Most dialects I hear onstage aren't very well done or congruent with others, and a dialect coach is often too expensive. I am, however, amazed by a side benefit. Actors using them are often freer physically, less self-conscious, and more nearly "someone else." Why? It almost seems that the part of their brain involved in moderating their speech forces them out of themselves. So, here's an eccentric tip. If you're really having trouble with a role early in the process, ask the director if you may play it in dialect for one rehearsal. It's a way of shaking yourself awake inside the skin of the role, a way to jump-start yourself. If a genial director allows you to experiment (no, you're not going to open with a dialect), what dialect should you use? Anything you're really comfortable with. Yes, others may laugh and that's fine, but you also may feel opened up to a character who before seemed a bad fit. Worth a try.

THE BOLT

We see people walk out of the room, meander out of the room, hurry out of the room, slide unobtrusively out of the room, but don't forget *the bolt* out of the room. Or even into the room for that matter. It used to be an English phrase, remember? "Where's Harry?" "Sorry, he's bolted." Now bolting anywhere for anything might basically be described as purposeful panic. You're in the kitchen eating grapes, and you suddenly remember you left the baby in the car a half hour ago when you unloaded the groceries. What do you do? You bolt. You're late for a crucial presentation. You hurry out to the bus stop, and then remember you've left your notes at home. You bolt back into the house. "The bolt" is obviously a high-stakes moment used for either dramatic or comic ends. It's explosive, it's sudden, it's purposeful and dramatic. Got a place for one?

THE ECSTATIC SPIN

Let's take a moment away from heavier matters to consider a trick that's probably been around since Thespis. I've seen this used by Laurence Olivier, Julie Harris, and scores of workaday actors. What is it? At a moment of high emotion, usually positive, when words won't do or aren't available and a sense of triumph or celebration pervades, the actor spreads his arms like wings and twirls in place, over and over until those watching feel dizzy with the actor's euphoria. It seems a gesture of pure joy and is usually unlike any other moment in the play. Related to ecstatic dancing, like the dervishes, it seems timeless and beautiful as well as being a spiritual state. It's yours now. Surely you'll find a moment to use it at least once in your career.

PRECISION

Precision is an interesting acting tool. The question is when to use it. A woman enters, she tosses two books onto her desk, flips her keys neatly over the sofa into a basket on her coffee table, kicks her shoes off her feet into a closet ten feet away, looks at her watch, points at the phone, it rings, and she sits, saying hello and picking it up simultaneously. Is this acting or circus technique? Both. Audiences adore precise physicality and business. They eat it up. It's particularly apt in comedy and productions that are highly styled. It's less useful in realist drama, unless the precision is a character trait. Precision, however, takes the stage. It commands attention, and when used inappropriately, reeks of overstated technique. So, precision is used to reveal character or to flat out entertain as a gimmick. It has a mechanical heart, so don't use it when something else is the point. Someone once said that psychology prevents precision, but precision can also muddle psychology. Everything in its place.

EASY TALKING

Words come easily, flowingly, and comfortably to some people and to others . . . well . . . they don't. Vocabulary often slips our mind only to be plucked from the void at the last moment. Sometimes the words we have aren't the words we want. And then there are the moments when we just don't know what to say. I've seen plays where everyone seemed to say everything they meant exactly as they wished to say it. Boy, it wasn't any planet I'd ever lived on. Yes, some plays have easier talkers than others. Shaw for instance, but even the immortal Shakespeare would recognize the battle to say what you mean. This gap between intent and language provides the listener with insight into the character and creates important tension. Some talking's easy and some isn't. Is that apparent in the role you're playing? Don't become a glib disc jockey of the soul.

MOVEMENT DEMONSTRATES PSYCHOLOGY

What physicality makes our state of mind visible? Does she sit so she won't attract attention? Does she refuse to sit at the head of the table because she fears responsibility? Does he go into the kitchen a dozen times to check the turkey because he's insecure? Does he move slowly to the door to show he doesn't care? Does he continually brush off his clothes because he fears he's unattractive? You get the point. How can the blocking and your behavior reveal feelings? Don't leave it all to the director; you probably know more about the character's internal life than she does. Spend an evening thinking about the character's fluid psychology as movement. As we all handle ourselves differently in space, the use of space reveals the mind and its preoccupations. Put your feelings in space and behavior. Acting is often mind and heart made visible.

DIMENSION

THE CENTRAL EQUATION

The mind is revealed in the words. Both are revealed in the body. All are transformed by the emotion. This forms a circle of connections so that it becomes impossible to tell where the starting point was. What we know is that the mind, the body, the words, and the emotions are always present as a single entity. Disconnect them at your peril.

MIDSTREAM

Usually onstage we see something we never see in life. Actors finish whatever they start. It's all so irretrievably tidy and responsible and unlikely. Simply on behalf of seeming a little more lifelike, let's pick a half-dozen moments in the role where you don't finish what you start. Better yet, let's stop in the middle. You start looking for your car keys in your pocket, but you stop in the middle of the search and get lost in thought about . . . whatever. You go to the refrigerator for a slice of cake. You reach out and grab the handle, but you never open it because you decide to go read *War and Peace* instead. Enjoy yourself! What else can you half finish and never complete in this role? Start, stop, digress. Or start, stop, start again. The idea of getting a new idea in the middle of something looks and feels spontaneous. It intrigues the audience with what you're suddenly thinking of and, lest we forget, seems a whole lot like our own lives.

IMPERSONATION

No, I'm not talking about your fabulous William Faulkner imitation that rolls people at parties in the aisle. I'm talking about basing a role on behaviors or vocal patterns you remember from your eccentric biology teacher in tenth grade. Don't knock it. Don't say it's artificial or technical or otherwise demeaning. It's a damn good idea used sparingly. For one thing, it's a reward for listening to all the acting teachers who told you to be observant. Here are some ground rules:

1. Don't pick up something the person observed does *all* the time. It will drive us crazy.
2. It's best to crib from two people simultaneously. It feels more like art than stealing.
3. Make sure it serves a purpose. "He always rubs his thumb and forefinger together *when he's thinking.*"
4. Choose for your model someone you think is ultimately charming, not irritating.
5. Whatever it is, don't do it more than two or three times in a scene.

Such stealing is honorable work. The best do it.

GET SOME FRUSTRATION INTO THE SCENE

It may sound ludicrous but honestly it's the actor's friend. There are two major ways to let it spice your acting. First, we have the frustration the character feels when she wants something very badly indeed and it is very very difficult to get. This sort of frustration very often leads the character into doing the wrong thing and thus making it even harder to achieve her goal. Wonderful! Doing the wrong thing then makes the character angry with herself and thus adds another dimension. The second category of frustration is minor but still fabulous. He wants her to marry him, and when he goes over to ask her, he notices he has pizza sauce on his shirt. This minor frustration in a major situation adds detail, dimensions, and (last but certainly not least) something to do. Experiment with both forms of frustration by adding a dollop to a scene that seems flat and no fun to play. It adds an odd sparkle.

A THING

Sometimes we move past the golden moment without even knowing it's there. The potential jewel often arrives within reach spontaneously while our mind is elsewhere. Yesterday, in a love scene, I saw one actor touch another actor on the arm. The second actor shook off the touch almost brutally, literally pushing his hand away rudely. This action provided a great opportunity for the rejected actor, but he didn't even notice. Why? The actor was looking beyond the present moment. He had an agenda not a consciousness. Perhaps he had other points he planned to make, and this explosive moment in the relationship (try slapping your husband's hand away and see if it gets remarked on!) just wasn't on the creative checklist. The actor needs a double-mind. One half has a plan, an action, and is pursuing it; the other half is open and aware to what is currently happening and realizes it must be incorporated and dealt with. Make sure you bring both minds to rehearsal. Don't walk past the golden nuggets on your way to somewhere else.

FINDING THE ATTACK IN DEFENSE

I was working on a scene last week where the husband finds a phone message his wife has scribbled with a man's name and hearts drawn under it. Fearing she's having an affair, he confronts her (she isn't). As soon as he attacked her, demanding she tell him what's going on, she chose a defensive position, seemingly flustered and trying to jolly him out of his mood. What would happen if she had attacked instead of defended? What if she let him know in no uncertain terms that he had *no* business prying into her phone calls and that his assumptions were demeaning to both of them? As soon as she attacked instead of defended, the scene seemed enriched, more complex, even more theatrical. What we need to remember is to examine the possibility of attack in what looks like a defensive situation. Is this always correct? Absolutely not. What is important is that we try the option to see what it produces. There are some actors who habitually prefer defense, and, frankly, it limits their casting. See if you can't find some attack in the scene.

THE TEASE

In strip clubs "the tease" is a piece of craft-oriented vocabulary. Let's change the context to the theater. When the line coming up will unravel the mystery, change the course of the story, set in motion the comedy or tragedy, use the tease. When the audience is dying to see or know, take a moment before you give it to them. Will she marry him, yes or no? Time for the tease. Did the butler do it? Time for the tease. Claudius is praying. Will Hamlet kill him? Time for the tease. Will Hedda really burn her lover's manuscript as she holds it near the flames? Tease! The key here is the audience's investment in the prior moment. Come on, be a little trashy, get them leaning forward in their seats. For some reason, we as actors routinely miss these possibilities. Perhaps it's because we spend a good deal of energy shutting the viewer out of our consciousness. Perhaps we think it's too brazen or gimmicky. Hey, maybe it's generous and theatrical. Tease me.

FIGHTING FOR CONTROL

A lot of times when you watch actors, they are either playing very in control or very out of control. What they are missing is all the shadings and possibilities of fighting for control. Keep an eye on your own life; this is something we do a lot. Your boyfriend has said something really demeaning that he meant as humorous, but you're at dinner with his parents. Ordinarily you'd let him have it, but now all you can do is seethe and try to pass off the moment lightly to his mom. Good acting moment. It's a little different than Stanislavski's idea of "keeping the lid on," because quite often we are trying not to let the others see the tumult we're feeling. Sometimes we do it by taking out these feelings on an activity— for example, we cut up the apples as if we were cutting up our boyfriend, but we try to cover it all with a smile. The character has to realize that there is something she wants that can't be achieved by setting these feelings and impulses free. Where are you fighting for control in your current play?

THE LIGHTBULB IN
THE COMIC STRIP

One thing and only one thing is true: This is the only acting book you can buy that uses Popeye as an example. Now, Popeye, by himself, is loading refrigerators on a truck. It gets harder. Popeye can't understand why he's struggling. Suddenly a lightbulb appears over his head. Popeye realizes he hasn't been eating his spinach! He gets it, and hopefully you get it. Where are these moments of sudden clarity in the role? The acting value is often the *suddenness*. It's a flash of understanding that strikes home with real physical participation. How could your character have missed this before? He shakes his head, throws himself back in the chair, and then rises performing a little impromptu dance. By God, he knows what to do now! Mark the lightbulb moments; look for them and enjoy playing them. I'm not talking about making a comic book of your performance—the moment can be large or small. I just don't want you to miss the opportunity. And, lest we forget, it helps to tell the story.

NOT BIGGER, FULLER

I'm amazed how often in class young actors express the fear that they are "doing too much." They ask with a small shudder, "It's not cheesy, is it? It's not hammy?" The most amazing thing is that nine times out of ten when they ask these questions, they are actually underplaying. "We don't want to be shouting all the time. We don't want to overdo it," at the very time when it's underdone. The point has nothing to do with how loud it is or the size of the gesture. The point is playing the moment richly and giving it full weight. The point is understanding the circumstances that surround the moment and the character's needs. The point is pursuing the action as if you really needed something. If you took videos of these same students worrying about being "cheesy" as they went about their lives, you would be surprised by the large scale of their personalities. If the line is "I'm telling you, she shot her husband," you don't think about size; you think about communicating this amazing fact. Fully!

TWO PATHS

Every speech your character has falls into two categories: 1. Your character knows what she wants to say and marshals her rhetorical devices and subclauses to support her major point, which she knew she was going to make from the very beginning. In other words, she has a point to make and she makes it. 2. Your character finds out what she means as she talks. She may start with a feeling and then suddenly and, to her, surprisingly makes a point or a connection. This character finds out where she is going while she goes. All acting is either one or the other. Look through your character's speeches and divide them into these two camps. Each results in a different kind of acting. We all use both these structures, sometimes within five minutes, but you, the actor, have to decide which is which. Usually the very structure of the line decides you. These, you say looking at the script, are all supporting evidence, and this is her point. She knew where she was going. Or the opposite. Just decide.

ONE THING AT A TIME

Mark Jenkins does an exercise he calls slow-talking. The idea is that you say the line and then let it breathe and occupy the space allowing your mind and heart to fill up the silence rather than quickly moving on, and moving on, and moving on. My version of that is taking one thing at a time. If the line is "What are you thinking? Why are you sitting there like that? Don't you understand what's going to happen?" It could be spoken in a rapid bunch with the single idea that the speaker needs advice and all three lines are a restatement of that need. Or you could let each line find its own need and weight before moving on to the next. Ask the question "What are you thinking?" and really expect an answer before moving on. "What's going to happen?" seems to be another crucial question, and the answer might change the speaker's direction or behavior. Use it. Use the moment where the answer should be and isn't. By giving these moments full weight, you may transform the final sentence.

TIK TOK

As a kid I loved the Oz books (there were at least thirty-six) and had particular affection for Tik Tok, the mechanical man. Both his brain function and movements had to be separately wound up. Nowadays he just reminds me of an acting problem. I was watching an audition yesterday and thinking how mechanical the actor's work seemed. What is mechanical acting? It's acting that has become lifeless through exact repetition: He made the gesture yesterday, now he's making it today. The energy in the mechanical performance seems to be expended in replication. The focus is not on the situation; it's on the presentation. Rhythms tend to be steady. Every line seems to have the same weight and importance. Eyes seem fixed. Gesture is sculpted. There are no real transitions from one idea to another. The body functions but seems devoid of impetus or impulse. The net effect matches the Oz character: It talks, it moves, but it's definitely not human. My dear actor friend, leave Tik Tok in Oz.

LEANING IN, LEANING OUT

Abstractly, we're always moving emotionally toward or away from the other character in the scene. We want to influence or are influenced or else we wish to avoid, to remain invulnerable. During one rehearsal, you might want to make this physical and visible (nobody need know but you). You'll actually, physically, lean in or move toward, or lean out and move away, as the psychology flows through the text. Doing this will bring the character's need to influence or avoid into your body as well as your thought process and will give you a new physical awareness of the character's moment-by-moment state. In a way, it's an actor's game of hot and cold. Although you may keep only a small percentage of these impulses in your final product, it can be very revealing. If you have no instinct to lean in or out, you will discover that the scene demands further work and thought.

ABSOLUTE VACILLATION

Yes, there are a few roles (damn few) where your character sets his course and pursues it to its conclusion like an arrow to the bull's-eye. The reason there are so few is it doesn't make for very interesting acting. My suggestion is to create a character who often questions his assumptions and goals. You don't want to play exactly the same in the second scene as you did in the first, right? Moments of self-evaluation and readjustment provide delicious acting changes that add a new layer of complexity. Where is that moment when a new thought creates a new action and a new direction? What's more fun for an actor than the moment when a certainty is smashed to smithereens? Better still is the series of moments when we pursue a goal, question it, give it up, try something else, and then, chastened, go back to our original idea. Remember *The Zoo Story* where the character says, "Sometimes we have to go a long way out of our way to come back a short distance correctly"? Well, the audience likes to watch that. Get off the superhighway and show us the twists and turns of the back roads.

ENTERTAINING

The very idea of getting up in front of people to tell a story is potentially terrifying. The idea that these same people would pay money to watch and listen could freeze the actor/storyteller in her tracks. Whatever the nature of the story, whether it's *Lear* or *Oklahoma!*, we have to face the fact that we are the evening's entertainment. Scary. What makes us worth the price of admission? What I have found to be the most stageworthy and theatrical weaponry in the actor's arsenal is simply concentration, belief, and thought process. Commit to those three parts of the work fully, and you are worth the price of admission. No ifs, ands, or buts. Audiences are still amazed and gratified by the actor's ability to seemingly live a life inside the narrative. All the other theatricalities—the juggling, the dancing, the tumbling, the wild gesticulation, the cocky presentation and vocal pyrotechnics—are all sideshows, but the three already mentioned are the main event. In a sense, these basics are the pyrotechnics. Strange but true.

LEAVING ROOM FOR THE ACTING

An actor friend once told me after a couple of drinks that acting is what you're feeling about what you're saying. Now sometimes the feeling is simultaneous with the saying, and sometimes it's provoked or deepened by the saying. In the latter case, you are plain old going to leave some space in all the talking for the feeling to emerge. I remember reading that the eminent English director Peter Hall once told Albert Finney, during a production of *Hamlet*, that he needed to pull back the headlong energy to leave some room to examine the text. High-energy actors particularly need to heed this advice because they sometimes drive so hard that there is no room for the character to reflect on the proceedings. Reflection. Where are the moments when it's crucial to the character you're playing? And decision making. Surely every choice he makes can't be made on the fly? Hold your horses! Don't let the part run away with you. You're riding hell for leather right past the feeling.

MORE IDEAS

I have often worked with a great American set designer whose models are so beautiful, so detailed,
so time-consuming, and so expensive that it's almost
impossible to bring oneself to say, "No, I don't think
that's right." Or, if you are so brave, I can't imagine saying no to the second model as well. The very
extraordinary nature of these models limits the free
exchange of ideas and creativity. The actor often
finds herself in an analogous situation with the director. In pursuit of a solution to a moment in rehearsal, she tries something, and it is rejected by this
august personage. She tries again and is once more
denied. At this point the actor is loathe to try again
and dumbly waits for the director's solution. Don't.
Part of the actor's warrior mentality lies in creating
a third solution and a fourth. You must accept no
from your editor, but you must step to the plate
again and again. As they say in the self-help books
on salesmanship: No is the beginning of Yes.

THE ONE-IDEA SYNDROME

This is about the good idea turned into a bad idea through overuse. Ellen has discovered Armand, who she is dating, is a drug dealer. He comes to propose to her not knowing she's going to break it off. The actor playing Ellen assumes she is now physically frightened of Armand. When he enters, she moves behind the sofa. She moves away when he moves forward. She doesn't look him in the face. Her hand shakes when she holds out the wineglass. Enough already. This idea is now overpowering the scene and reducing its complexity. Usually these ideas that are taken too far are excellent responses to the circumstances, but because they are defendable and interesting to play, we extend them well past the time when they have made their point. The audience is likely to feel their overstatement as a kind of hectoring and become irritated by the repetition. Add something else. She's frightened but still attracted plus she's surprised by the proposal. Now the work seems dimensional. Always have more than one idea playing.

ACTION/ACTIVITY

What we're looking for is an activity that expresses the action. If you want Jane to leave the house forever, you might pack a suitcase for her while you revile her for making a pass at your boyfriend. The action might also be accompanied by an activity that is also a metaphor. If you feel poor Jane has broken faith with you, you might take a hammer to the gifts she has given you as you let her have it verbally. In the scene when you declare your love for Ralph, you might draw a charcoal portrait of him while you explain your feelings. Once you have discovered a powerful action for a beat or a scene, you creatively search for an activity that enhances it. Sometimes the activity expresses subtext: The conversation is about rewiring a house, but the real tension concerns committing to having a child, and the activity is knitting a child's sweater. You know the action. Now discover the activity.

THE GLASS

Now here's an acting use for an old saw. Does the character you're playing see the glass of his life as half empty or half full? This tilt of the balance toward the negative or positive can create some interesting playing. It's intriguing to see the half-full people confront the bad news and the half empty, the good news. The point isn't simple negativity or optimism (who wants to see that character?), it's the challenges life provides to either attitude. I've seen wonderful comic turns based on a character finding a silver lining to catastrophe after catastrophe. "Well, since the car's totaled, we won't have to worry about that oil change." Knowing the basic tropism of the character can guide you toward a surprising acting approach and provide an unusual moment that might otherwise seem obvious. Read the script again to see which camp this character seems to fit in. What would happen if you played him the other way? It can get your juices flowing.

IRONY AND THE ACTOR

Probably better begin with the definition, huh? Irony is the use of words to express something different from and often opposite to their literal meaning. We immediately recognize this as an actor's tool, yes? Obviously, it's particularly useful in sophisticated contemporary comedy (and Molière!). Some actors have ironic natures and find such values in every text they work on. These actors can move on to the next tip. The rest of us have to decide if this particular character is a vehicle for the ironic view. If not, there might still be moments that employ it. On the simplest level it becomes a commentary on other characters, as in: "Oh, absolutely, he *loves* me [and it's destructive]," or "He has a sense of humor all right [and it's truly stupid]." The character may also have an ironic view of the situation she finds herself in, having accepted a weekend invitation from people she dislikes only to find them celebrating her. Read the role for ironic possibilities. The result may surprise you.

REACTING INSTEAD OF DECIDING

We've talked about "taped" lines (you've decided how to say them), but oh my, how about "taped" reactions? Sarah is told by William that her prized ferret is dead. As she did yesterday and the day before that and the day before that, she drops her venetian glass goblet, makes a horrified O of her mouth, and sits heavily on the packing box. As a matter of fact, she's done that in every rehearsal and performance for weeks. No doubt about it, that reaction is dead, mummified, technical, and contentless. Only the very, very best actors can do the same reaction over and over and keep it filled with interior life and the illusion of spontaneity. The rest of us are going to have to be brave enough to vary what we do. To break such a habitual moment, try doing less or, better still, nothing. Then, the next time through, tell yourself you have no idea what you'll do and let it simply happen. Or, do it ten different ways in rapid succession and pick one on the spur of the moment. Remember, we see you, and dead is dead.

SET GOALS FOR THE RUN-THROUGH

Having watched actors in the run-through process for forty years, I find they are vague about the specific value. Actors enjoy run-throughs—they need them certainly—but usually they have only a vague sense of "how they did." They tend to categorize these events as "good" or "bad" and speak generally, saying, "I just wasn't present" or "I felt like I was shouting too much" or "I liked the first act, but the second act sucked." I suggest that the actor make a battle plan for each run-through. Take a few minutes and decide what you're working on and what you want to accomplish in the next run. Include a target scene you feel is shaky and has a specific problem and decide how you will attack it tomorrow. This plan is ten or fifteen minutes well spent because it gives you a basis for judging the day's work. Otherwise, you have only the director's notes to provide an analysis, and she may not be focused on you or may react generally rather than specifically. Be proactive.

THE VALUE OF USING
THE WRONG FORK

Manners: agreed-upon behavior to allow social interaction. So much of the acting work we do is built around manners. We take off our hat in the house without even thinking about it. Obviously, manners change from culture to culture, so the first thing is to understand what manners, mores, and social graces are operative in your play. Does your character know, have, and value the appropriate behavior? Is he aware that when bowling you don't make your approach at the same time as someone in the next lane? If he knows the rules, does he follow them or break them? Sometimes a defining moment is when the character doesn't or won't take off that hat. It can work both ways. You kiss a woman you only met five minutes ago, or you take off your shoes unasked in someone's home. The actor can build interesting, even telling, moments inside or outside the accepted norm. Which side is your character on, and why?

SMALL CHANGES

No matter how precise your performance has become through repeated rehearsals, no matter how many performances you have played, no matter how demanding the director, your work must remain a living thing, and living things change. You are going to have new ideas, instincts, and perceptions eight performances in. How do you know what change is allowable? Let's put it this way, the structure remains, the details change. Blocking is structure; it stays as it has been decided unless the director notes otherwise. Anything you do that the other actor has become dependent on for the structure of her performance stays. The text, obviously, stays as it is. Fights and big emotional moments with others onstage maintain their structure. The intent and function of the performance remains. But a line reading here, a gesture there, small touches of blocking, and the handling of props can change. These are living things proceeding from living, changeable consciousness. You need those changes to stay alive.

CHANGING THE MUSICAL NOTE

Sorry to seem so technical, but our century, long focused on the psychological, has sometimes made us
aurally incompetent. Young actors in my classes
often speak text on the same musical note for far
too long. Tonalities are not lost on the audience.
They hear the music of the text as well as its meaning. This implies that if the other actor has established and sustains loud, you can get your share of
the stage with soft. A useful generality would be that
you should never bring your line in on the same musical note that the person before you has closed with.
Come in above or below. In any case, it helps to get
out of your head and really listen to what sort of
tonal and rhythmic work is going on so you can
make your contribution to the jazz and not the mo-
notony. Focusing only on psychology can cause you
to forget the simple fact that you're not a solo;
you're playing in an orchestra. Where's your note?

HOW TO BE SAVED FROM
THE BIG IDEA

We're not speaking about the play's idea here, we're speaking of the actor's "big idea" about the role. Anyone who has acted has had these ideas, and it's not a good idea. They go like this: "I think that this father is descended from the archetypical father in the commedia, so I'll use commedia poses in the role" or "Tartuffe reminds me of Southern evangelists, so I'll use the vocal pattern they do." These "big ideas" often reduce the complexity of a good role and, in effect, flatten it out and turn it all one color. If you, for instance, walk a certain way or talk a certain way, it very often draws the audience's attention away from the circumstances and even the story of the scene. It can make the actor less responsive to others because the "big idea" limits the reactions possible. It is, I think, better for the actor to define creativity as a series of subtle shifts based on the action, the obstacle, and the other actors' performances. The great performance is seldom a big idea. It is usually a thousand congruent small ones.

TWO THINGS

Everything about acting seems easier and more interesting when you're choosing between two possibilities. Hmmm, I could do this or this! While you're making choices as an actor, conceive an alternative you could toss into the mix. It gives both you and the character decisions to make and thus creates thought process. "Should I sit down next to her, which creates intimacy, or over here, which takes the pressure off?" "Should I cajole or demand?" Often the actor selects an idea out of the air and acts on it without realizing that idea could also generate a second choice with a very different outcome. See a possibility and ask yourself "What's the alternative?" The other value is that it heightens the sense of "the first time" and gives the work an edge. Don't be satisfied with the first idea. Use it as a crowbar to pry out another. Work with two, try both. It's almost a definition of rehearsal.

THE RED NOSE

The clown hides behind it and feels free. What should you use? Well, situation and circumstance of course. The more you know, the freer you feel. But at the very beginning when you're first on your feet, some version of the red nose can put you at ease until you know more. Find simple actions you know you can complete, such as tying your shoes or picking up crumbs off a table. Hide behind those. Choose a characteristic stance, a posture for sitting and something to nibble on that you keep about your person. Hide behind those. Now, you may dispense with these little securities later. They may eventually prove to be too obvious or too limiting, but never feel you have to apologize for using them to get through the first few days. Give yourself things to fiddle with in your pockets until more meaningful props emerge. Hide behind those. I knew one actor who said he always carried a little puzzle in his pocket. "It's so I have something to do until I know what to do." A little hiding is quite respectable.

TEXT

MINDFULNESS

There is a negative actor's mind-set that believes the audience is interested in the actor rather than the story. The actor, believing this, feels he must perform prodigiously to justify that interest. The actor justifying, pursues a course of being more energetic, more amazingly physical, funnier, wilder, faster, louder, and sexier than the audience has ever seen before. The result is usually like the seven-year-old doing anything for attention but lacks the seven-year-old's innocence and charm. The positive actor's mind-set is mindful of his role in the story, the current circumstances in which the character finds himself, the goals (actions) he must pursue to allow the story's fruition, and how to blend his acting into the chain of action/reaction. Allow the story to be the star of the endeavor. This regard for the story I would call the actor's mindfulness. It is a challenging but modest mind-set that allows us to differentiate between acting and showing off. Such a course, pursued fully, is also satisfyingly theatrical.

CLOSE ENOUGH FOR GOVERNMENT WORK

There is a class of actors who has the theatrical equivalent of perfect pitch. They innately, and usually not consciously, know how they should sound and behave in any scene. They back up this active intuition with good technique. They are confident; they move well; they can deliver on demand a close approximation of any emotion. You want angry? They got angry. You want angry with a tinge of regret and affection? No problem. The problem is there isn't any there there. It's generic, not individual. The actor is distanced from the effect she is producing at the very moment she produces it. Worse, it's addictive, and these actors can't stop doing it, because it's almost good and it's well crafted. At a casting call, where no one is perfect, they often get hired as the next best thing. Now, if you fall into this category, take the cure. The cure lies in your being willing to make yourself vulnerable onstage, vulnerable and specific. Do the following: Slow down and be truly present. Try to discover what you personally would do in the situation. Don't manufacture emotion; break your flow, go back over the given circumstance, try to be *with* the other actor. Allow yourself not to know what you'll do next. Something genuine and surprising will happen.

CLARITY

Sometimes we don't need fabulous, explosive, wildly imaginative acting. Sometimes we don't need powerful emotion from the deepest human well. Sometimes we just need the actor to make a complicated speech or situation *clear.* I sit in theaters across the land and watch actors ladle emotion over flailing physicality, and all I can think is "*What* are they *saying?*" First, before you personalize or raise the stakes, just make sure you really know what the speech means. What's its point? How is the speech structured? Does the speaker already know the point when she starts, or does she find it as she speaks? Is the speech a carefully integrated piece of logic or a scattershot tour of her fractured emotional state? What's the relationship of the last line of the speech to the speech as a whole? If she repeats phrases, why? Is it a series of illustrations of a single point? Remember the phrase "What's your point?" Ask it of the speech, then decide how the acting builds to it.

THE HOT CENTER

In every scene there is an animating need or dilemma that underpins everything that happens. The characters don't necessarily talk about it all the time, but it remains present and not behind any digression. No matter what the actors talk about in the scene, they feel the presence of this central need and problem. In *Crimes of the Heart*, Lennie has always had a crush on Doc, but he only has eyes for her sister Meg. When he comes to tell Meg that her horse has been killed, the scene has many elements, but Lennie's attraction to him, which is never spoken of, is always present. This is the hot center of the scene, and the actors' awareness of it provides the scene's engine. Find the hot center, and then relate as many moments in the scene to it as you can. This is not only the glue that holds the scene together, but its energy source. Without it, we have only a series of moments of varying interest. With it, everything relates and gains power. Seek it. Use it.

BETRAYING THE ACTION

A quick review. How are we defining an action? What you want the other person to do, to feel, or to understand. What unit is crucial to playing an action? The beat. What is a beat? A beat is a series of lines dealing with one topic either textual (they are talking about pineapple plantations) or subtextual (underneath the pineapples, they are really discussing their failed marriage). There is thus one action per beat. Can you have the same action for several beats? No, but you may have the same superobjective. What's a superobjective? What your character wants above all. Your superobjective may be to become the world's greatest tap dancer, but the current action is to get your mother to loan you $10,000. You betray the action by deciding the same goal can cover several consecutive beats. It flattens out your performance, makes the work feel repetitive, and stops your work from moving forward. Reexamine the beats, adjust the action, and give yourself a new lease on life.

NAMING THE BEATS

All right, to review, a beat is the theatrical version of the paragraph. It is not seen from one character's point of view. A beat changes when what is being talked about, objectively or subtextually, changes. Usually in my work I indicate the beats with brackets:

[~ ~ ~ ~ ~ ~ ~ ~ ~

~ ~ ~ ~ ~ ~ ~ ~ ~]

Now, I'm suggesting you name the beat to show you have absorbed what it's about. If the beat is about going bowling, I'm not suggesting you call it "bowling." What's it really about? It might be called "flirtation," it might be called "establishing dominance," it might be "escaping reality." The point is that you, the actor, have to realize what is really going on here to give your acting specificity. After you've been naming the beats for a while, it becomes much clearer what is really going on with your character and what is the nature of his relationships. Very often you discover that beats can't be simply taken at face value. The naming will surprise you.

SHAPE

Because our theater became so deeply psychological and we have balanced that with the flamingly theatrical, we tend not to study speech structure. How is this speech shaped?

1. What's it about? What is it trying to say?
2. Does it have a thesis? A moment where it declares its intent or subject?
3. Is part of the speech support material for that thesis?
4. Is there a summation where the speech's point is restated or declared?
5. What does the speech build toward? How is it structured to do that?
6. Can you outline the speech?

Once the actor penetrates and understands the structure, it often unblocks her emotionally as well as intellectually. There is usually a structure, and that makes certain demands on the actor. A little analysis will free your spontaneity.

WHAT YOU DON'T HAVE TO DO

What we all have to remember is that a well-written script makes it unnecessary to emphasize certain things. Richard III, for heaven's sake, is so evil that we don't need to play it. Romeo and Juliet are such attractive, sweet, charming, and involving roles that we needn't push those qualities. I recently directed a play in which one father's son was a school shooter and the other's son, the victim. We inherently sympathized so keenly with these two men that the actors didn't need to play for sympathy; it was guaranteed by the text. If the actor plays what the script already provides, audience members feel that the performers don't trust them or, worse, that they are being treated like kindergartners who may "miss the point." Read your script carefully so that you can see what the playwright has already done for you. Now you're free to work in the less overt areas or deliver those sides of the role that may be a tad underwritten and unspoken.

WHAT'S ALIENATION THEORY?

Let's oversimplify. It's forcing the audience to think about what's happening instead of simply being swept along by story and emotion. How does an actor do that? By adopting an ironic tone, by playing to the audience instead of to the other actor, by clarifying and teaching a point rather than embedding it in the role's psychology, by playing text and physicality as two separate tracks unrelated to each other, by adopting a mechanical physicality and tone, by playing a critique of the character rather than the character itself. It has to do with wanting the audience to think not simply feel. When does an actor employ these techniques? When study of the author's style and intent seem to demand it or when the director chooses to apply these techniques to the material. Does this imply a different relationship to character? To a degree. It assumes you want to communicate or "show" the audience members something about the character rather than allow them to take what they will. If for instance the character is seen to represent the negative characteristics of materialism, those characteristics *are* the character.

DON'T DEFANG DANGER

I was recently watching tapes of TV's *Sopranos* and became aware how dangerous most of the conversations were. Say the wrong thing and you could end up in the East River. Even ordinary conversation was a minefield. No wonder this show penetrates the national psyche. When language is potentially dangerous, it's dramatic by definition. Allow the fact of needing to tread carefully in most conversations to spice your work. Look at not only what you should say in a given scene but what you shouldn't. When is this character's dialogue treading on others' toes? The actor who hasn't spent a little time studying the needs of the other characters he interacts with often overlooks these verbal grenades. Did your character say that wittingly or unwittingly? Does calling her a "charming slut" amuse her or infuriate her? And did your character consider the difference? The language is often where the conflict lies. Don't overlook it.

THE MESSAGE

Sometimes it doesn't hurt to think a little bit about what you're delivering. What are you saying to the audience through the role? I know, I know, our concentration is basically kept onstage, but if you are willing to admit that the playwright wants the audience to think in certain ways about certain situations, then how do you contribute to that message? Your character is, on one hand, a three-dimensional psychology with certain characteristics and, on the other, part of a metaphor or a pointed tale that instructs us how or how not to live. Your character may embody this message as a positive or a negative. If, for instance, *Romeo and Juliet* teaches us about the centrality of love, what is Tybalt's point? Tybalt prefers honor to love and is willing to die for family or nation but not romance. All I'm saying here is that characters exist as elements of a larger story or message and that we, as actors, cannot ignore that part of our job. The message provides the limits within which we create.

THE TURN

The turn is the moment when the scene suddenly sets off in a new direction. Like a race car driver, the actor needs to see the turn and negotiate it. Let's say, for instance, a couple has been arguing about money, which brings up her father who has been giving them loans. The man says, "You're dependent on him in more ways than one. He practically dresses you for God's sake." The following conversation is no longer about money but about the larger issue of dependency. This new subject calls on different feelings and recalls different conversations they have already had. The tone changes; the tactics change. The two people relate differently to this subject than the previous one. They even play in a different rhythm. The actors need to understand there has been a turn and that something new is demanded of them. It sounds different, it feels different, it is different. If you don't make this turn, we lose touch with the narrative. Read the script again and hunt them out.

REALLY ASK THE QUESTION

Actors sometimes run question marks like rural red lights. Go through your part and underline the questions as if you really wanted and expected an answer. Questions are a natural glue that tie the characters in a scene together. Where you fail to want the answer, you fail to include the other actor. Curiosity is an attractive character trait and an acknowledgment that we are not alone. Also keep your eyes open for a question placed in the middle of your speech. That's the one that tends to get lost. The actor knows that, because of the construction of the line, the question will not be answered, but your character *does not*. You ask the question, the other character doesn't answer, and you understand something new about the situation because of her avoidance. Start by asking each question with a real sense of demand. By seemingly demanding an answer, you demand a reaction, verbal or nonverbal, and the scene deepens.

THE IMPERATIVE

The imperative is the moment when you have to know, have to have, have to prevail. These are the sentences that define your character's needs, and the needs tell us who the character is. These moments are definitely not requests. You identify them immediately through the vocabulary. These lines contain the words *I must, you must, I have to, I've got to, you can't.* They bear down on defining moments and relationships. They are the character's necessities, and you must act them as such. The vocabulary of the imperative implies and demands high stakes. These aren't things you simply want. They are things you must have. Go through the play and underline these imperatives. Very often they get overlooked when the actor has some momentum going. Sometimes it's simply a matter of emphasis.

THE MIDLINE PAUSE

I remember there was something indefinable in my father's acting that made his work unusual and individual (at least in my experience), and one night it came to me: He kept pausing to think in the middle of a sentence. In one sense it was a gimmick, a technique, but he used it well, usually placing the pause after the connective. Here's how it went: "Yes, I did tell your father that and [three- or four-beat pause] to give him credit, he took it well." "I don't give a damn what you think but [three- or four-beat pause] I still want you go to with me." He was careful always to place it at the moment when the character might need to frame the way he put something. Also he used it sparingly and was careful not to do it if it would spoil the play's rhythms or sense.

TO CONVINCE, TO DECIDE, TO UNDERSTAND

Most of our acting falls into these three categories and certainly most of our long speeches. Even knowing which of these voyages you are embarked on is a great help. If, for instance, it's a speech to convince, it usually has to knock over a couple of obstacles en route. Sometimes it has to demolish the other character's positions before pressing your own. If it's a speech to decide ("to be or not to be"), it usually runs down the virtues or failures implicit in taking this or that path. If it's a matter of understanding, it analyzes, separates, defines, and compares possible meanings. This "understanding" will probably lead to action crucial to the plot. Should you mistake one for another in the text, both the psychology and the narrative may become incomprehensible. So, before you turn the acting loose, take a long hard look at what the speech is structured to do.

WHAT'S FUNNY?

The sad truth is that we're not all natural comedians and yet the gods of casting may still occasionally slip us a comic role. What is the normally skilled actor who didn't inherit Jim Carrey's gene pool to do? Well, we might have to engage in a little analysis. (Don't tell the natural comics; they'll laugh us to scorn.) Sit down in your favorite chair with your favorite chips and consider what's funny about the role. What's funny scene by scene? Usually it's a dislocation: George is focused on ice for his drink while the world ends; Suzy is in love with George who is in love with her cat. Sometimes it's a misunderstanding: George thinks Bill (who he has found in his wife's closet) is a tax collector. Sometimes it's obsessive behavior: George spits whenever he sees the color blue. Whatever it is, you need to recognize the comic machinery, so you can focus on it and play it full out. If you're not a natural comedian, focus on situation, situation, situation. If you understand how it functions, you can get the laughs that are there.

GETTING THE ACTION
INTO THE WORDS

So we know we're supposed to be playing an action (what we want the other person to do, to feel, or to understand—some people call it the objective), but the problem in a lot of acting is that it never reaches the words. The line is, "Will you calm down for a minute so that we can actually have a negotiation?" In this situation, the other person has a fixed position, and if he maintains that, you won't get something crucial for you. The action is to get the other person to give a little so everyone gets a little. The action is to secure a negotiation. Now when you say the word *negotiation*, it has to *contain* your action. You have to fill the word *negotiation* with your need and longing. We could call it a matter of emphasis, but it's far more crucial. That word is a vehicle or container for your action. If we can't see and hear it in the word, we lose track of your need. When the words and your action come together, *fill* the words; otherwise the action lies dead in the water.

THE GORILLA ON THE TABLE

At this moment in the scene what is really being discussed? What's really at issue? Has it changed from the moment before, or is there just a distraction, and we'll get right back to it? She called him "rootless and undependable" and wanted to know where she really stood. Now they are discussing where to go for dinner, but her unanswered question about where she stands is still the gorilla on the table, and they both know it. Usually this gorilla is either a crucial question or need that demands a response. Sometimes it's unspoken but known to both parties. This gorilla stays in the minds and hearts of everyone present until it is dealt with or a larger gorilla shows up. For instance, her need to know where she stands might be superceded by his admission that he's seriously ill. In that case, we're dealing with a new gorilla. In theater, there is almost always an important issue in play. If you don't recognize what it is, you and the text have just parted company. Remember, often you start with issue A move on to subissues B and C, and then return to A with renewed vigor. Keep track. What's the gorilla?

WHAT'S THE MOST IMPORTANT LINE IN THE SPEECH?

Here's the nitty-gritty for the actor: Some things are more important than other things, and the acting is meant to make that clear. Now, how do we go about that? Well, we look for the text's central meanings all the way down to *this* speech's central meaning— and the lines that reveal or exemplify those meanings. Well, it's our job to pop them out. That which you deem important should strike directly to the heart of the play. When that happens, the line and the play's meaning cohere to give the moment extra weight and power. An actor who makes no real distinction between the wheat and the chaff renders the text inedible. The "door" seems as important as the "croissant" and the "croissant" seems as important as the "hand grenade" with which she plans to blow up her mother. By making everything important, we suck meaning from the play. Understanding the line's relationship to the play's meaning doesn't tell you *how* to play, but it illuminates the target you must hit.

THE FOREST FOR THE TREES

In the midst of a dozen interesting details, problems, and obstacles, have you lost track of the scene's *function?* You're playing Juliet. It's—what else—the balcony scene. OK. First, you're worried about getting hooked up with a Montague. Second, you're worried Tybalt will come out and make fish bait of Romeo. Third, you're worried Romeo thinks you're a pushover because he overheard how much you like him. Fourth, you're worried about how your mom and dad will take all this. Fifth, you're worried the whole relationship with Romeo is going too fast. Sixth, you're worried the nurse will overhear you, and you'll be grounded for a year. Altogether, you are very, very, very worried for very good reasons that are taken directly from the script. All these worries are making you very cranky with Romeo. You have lost track of the scene's function, which is to show two young people so crazy in love they would do anything to make it work. You have to meld the irritation *and* your love. As you and the director chart the scene, make sure you don't drift too far from the central function. Check it.

THE ACTOR'S TIME MACHINE

Yes, there is much to be said about playing "moment by moment" and "being in the moment," but remember, time intersects. Look through the scene. Where does the present moment collide with the character's or story's past? It may be when he realizes he is treating his new love much as he treated his ex-wife. Is it when she realizes how much like her mother she is? These past/present moments usually have strong story significance, emotional content, and lovely acting possibilities. Even better is the moment where the past impacts the present and endangers or enlightens the future. When Cousins in *Major Barbara* understands how the munitions maker Undershaft has become a power for good, he realizes that, for Barbara to love him in the present, he must become the Undershaft of the future. It's an ecstatic, unforgettable instant of theater created by time colliding. Comb the script for such moments. They are pure acting heaven.

FIRST THINGS FIRST

I've had a lot of bad ideas in my time and one of the latest was to devise forty-five separate categories for judging acting, which I planned to use as an analytical tool for helping students. When I attempted to put it into practice, I was immediately stymied by the fact that the categories were all linked and overlapping. I could not, for instance, separate rhythm from action, or transitions from obstacles. Ah well. But it did become clear that many of the categories were dependent on the superobjective. How can you play individual actions if you don't know what the character wants overall? How could you discern what you are pursuing in this moment or that moment if you haven't articulated a larger goal? Without the crucial need, how would you develop thought process or subtext? So, here's job number one, rule number one, the foundation, and the first principal all wrapped up in one: What's the major *want* (not just in this scene but in the play)? Now, what's the major want in the scene and how does that relate to the overall want? There is, believe me, nothing else you can do until that's clear to you.

DESCRIBING THE INDESCRIBABLE

You come home from the concert and Uncle Andy turns to you and says, "So what was the Brahms like?" How the hell are you going to describe that music to Uncle Andy so that he gets a sense of it? In a way, that's always the position the actor (or character) finds himself in. How can I describe these feelings to her? How can I describe the love I feel? How can I describe why I have to leave? Think of saying the lines as an endless attempt to describe the indescribable. In the play none of us wants to see, no one ever has to find the right words, they just say that damn text from beginning to end, no problem. In the play I want to see, the actor carves the language out of unforgiving rock. It takes effort and skill, and even when you say it the very best you can, the character knows that it's imperfect. It just doesn't quite describe Brahms's music. In the best acting, the character knows that language is an imperfect instrument. It always falls a little bit short of what's needed.

CHARACTER

SAVING SOMETHING

There is something your character never does. Whatever this is defines your character by its very absence. Now this thing that is absent will be released in your character by change or plot twist at the very end of the play. The question is, of course, what is it? Let's, for lack of a better term, call it the pivotal absence. It needs to be based deep in your character's needs and to somehow reveal the beating heart of the story being told. It might be a release of emotion dammed from the beginning of the play. It might be the smile always held back and absent until the moment of closure. It might be touching someone or something from which you have steadily kept your distance. This absence you are finally going to fill is also a metaphor for growth, decline, or important change. If you can find this sudden flowering, it can cap the role for you and the audience. What is that something in the role you're playing? What is this thing that isn't there?

CHARACTER THROUGH RELATIONSHIP

Yes, you could walk with a limp, continually eat pistachios, and develop a dynamite Missouri accent, but that's not really what character work is. Character, in the deepest sense, is explicated through relationships. How do you treat the other person? How do you expect to be treated by her? In what ways and with what limits do you express anger with this particular person? How do you curry favor with her? What is the nature of touch in this relationship? How do you dress for him? How do you set limits with him? In what ways are you prone to express weakness with him? What strengths does she assist? What does she do that drives you crazy? Make your own list. It is through these expressions of self in relationship to another that we come to know you. Work in those areas first. Then bring on the pistachios.

THE WHOLE THING

You got the role. You've read the script several times. You have the beginning of an idea about the author's intended meaning. How can you get a clear perspective on your part? Allow me to introduce you to my mother: "Well what I do, Jon, is to write out longhand every one of my lines in order without any of the other lines in between. First of all, it really helps me learn my lines, and you know I like to have them down very early in rehearsal. What I wanted to tell you, though, is that seeing my lines in that fashion really allows me to see what the part is and what it isn't. It dispels my fantasies about the part and brings home the realities. After doing this, I invariably find the part easier to understand and to act, and I stop trying to make it more than it is, which has always been my big fault. Try it with your part in *Merchant of Venice* and see if it doesn't help." (From a letter, January of 1957.)

CONFUSING FLIRTATION WITH SEXUAL TENSION

How many times, oh lord, have we had to sit through aggressive clichéd sexuality when what was wanted was simple flirting? It's a bonehead mistake and implies a lack of good sense and good taste. In addition it lacks that crucial quality, charm, and is often unlikable. It is a mistake often made by male directors working with female performers. Don't give me that look—it is. Flirtation is a sign that someone is signaling a desire for further contact and time spent with a person he is attracted to. It does not imply that sex is desired. Sexual signaling does. Are these two people ready for sex or do they want to get to know each other? Which does the text really demand? Don't mistake one for the other because the audience knows the difference and is dismayed when the choice seems mistaken or, as is usually the case, premature.

THE PRONOUNCED CHOICE

I was watching an actor in a new Arthur Miller play (still productive at eighty-six!) a week ago, and he had found a wonderful hangdog, bloodhound-who-didn't-get-dinner demeanor for the role that was riveting. His whole body seemed to hang in loose folds. He looked at everyone both hopefully and reproachfully at the same time. He looked, in fact, like a human being whose only wish was to have you pet him. It was riveting; you couldn't take your eyes off him. As the play developed, however, there were things the actor had to do and say that were difficult, nigh impossible, given the pronounced characteristics he had chosen. Beware. When you make the bold, seen-from-a-mile-away choice, make absolutely sure the play will allow you to function well within the box the bold choice has put you in. I might almost (but not quite) say "play the situation, not the character." Playing the situation will give you the character. It isn't quite true, but it's percentage baseball.

BEING SURPRISED

As we've said, you know what's coming, but your character doesn't. It's remarkable how often we are surprised in life and how seldom onstage. Allow yourself to be blindsided. What would you never have expected in a thousand years? Maybe an obstacle you hadn't seen coming bangs suddenly into you. Maybe the situation forces you to redirect your energy. Assumptions are destroyed by a piece of behavior. You're caught off balance and have to do it differently. It makes compelling moments. Remember, you're on page 65 and page 66 doesn't exist yet. Your character may project the future, but she damn well doesn't know it. Be startled, dumbfounded, caught unawares, made speechless. Respond hesitantly, even stupidly. We don't always handle surprises well. The surprises aren't always obvious; you may have to go looking for them.

LASCIVIOUS FUN

There are times when the theater wants to shock and offend as a way of dynamiting closed minds and critiquing social norms. There are other plays where, for reasons of keeping the focus on character or story, we try to soft-pedal profanity and sexuality. In these cases, there are techniques. I remember my father showing a young actor how to "bury" profanity through underemphasis and emphasizing other key words or inserting a piece of lightly distracting business that pulled focus from the line. When it comes to sexual innuendo or physically explicit business, the key is the good nature and even amusement with which it's executed. If the actors involved can let the audience know that they are comfortable and emphasize their likability and humor amidst the lustiness (particularly in comedy), the audience relaxes rather than becoming judgmental or offended. We want the audience to receive the play, not reject it. Choose carefully just how tough-minded you want such moments to be.

WHAT YOU'RE DOING NOW ISN'T SIMPLY WHAT YOU'RE DOING NOW

A danger in the acting process is to fall into what I call "rosary acting." This means you play one "bead" at a time without relating them. At the beginning of the play, you talked about how, above all, you hate it when people are two-faced. Now, in the final thirty minutes, you're making jokes about your fiancée secretly having lunch with her old boyfriend. What might be a small moment has a different tonality because of what was earlier established. You've stated your hatred of duplicity, and now you're laughing at your girlfriend's dishonesty; you're being illogical. What if your character realized his inconsistency right in the middle of that moment? Perhaps this little thing on page 57 is part of a much larger current of the role. A small moment might reverse a large trend. The character, a drinker, refuses wine at a party. Maybe it's a sign of something larger. Ask yourself, does this line or exchange have a larger resonance? A moment might be important not for what you do, but for what you choose not to do because of earlier behaviors we've seen. What's the heredity of this moment?

SITTING, STANDING, OR LOLLING

Before you get into any big-time physical characterization—"I think he sits and cuts himself with a steak knife whenever he watches television"—let's just start with the basics. Does she have a preferred posture or position when sitting? How about standing? Weight equally distributed? Feet close together or wide apart? What's his walk? Any small nervous habits when he's bored? You'll be amazed how quickly these everyday traits add up to a highly specific character. A half dozen will be more than you need and probably more than you'll have time to absorb or allow to become second nature. The smaller these character adjustments—the less noticeable in and of themselves—the more magically transformational they make your work. "I don't know how he did it, but that's an entirely different person!" Use the small and almost invisible to layer a physical characterization—not too much or too often. And never tell what.

PLAYING BRANDO'S KOWALSKI

Ask anyone, he or she will have a different opinion. If you're playing a role and there's a film made from the play, should you go down and rent it? If you're passing through Chicago and there's a production of a play you know you'll be doing next summer, should you go see it? I don't know if you should, but here's some advice if you do. Try to see what actions and what circumstances the actor is playing. Concentrate not on what he does but on *why* he's doing it. Concentrate on what the actor playing your role seems to want and need from his relationships. You could choose to play those wants and needs, but what you actually *did* would be quite different. Don't pay too much attention to the actor's physicality; if you took that home, it would be the beginning of imitation, but you can learn from what that actor seems to need. Later, you'll create that need with your own physicality and probably emphasize other circumstances. You bought the ticket; now find the why, not the how.

TAKING THE HIT

A lot of actors like to dish it out, but they don't like to take it. Remember, you're not playing a super-woman impervious to irony, sarcasm, and criticism. You need to be vulnerable, to bleed, to be hurt, to be thrown off balance, to realize you've just made a mistake or put something badly. You particularly need this dimension in characters that seem, most of the time, very much in charge of their circumstances. One of the keys here is listening so you're aware of the moment when someone has scored off your character, put his finger on your character's sore point. The second key lies in *not* deflecting the hit but in letting it land and have an effect on you. Taking the hit is humanizing and lends your character dimension. It gives you a chance to absorb rather than being endlessly (and eventually) irritatingly aggressive. Allow your character the opportunity to be wounded.

DOING THE WRONG THINGS

Your character isn't perfect. Sometimes she doesn't practice what she preaches. Sometimes she jumps to conclusions. Maybe patience or good taste eludes her. Possibly she unfairly takes her frustrations out on others. Could be she's a little greedy and a little self-centered. Looking for flaws in your character's character is sometimes a shortcut to getting inside the role. Some actors subconsciously need the audience's admiration and work to eliminate or play down character flaws, and what could have been a jagged study of good and evil becomes a whitewash. The interestingly flawed character intrigues the viewer and usually deepens the play (not if you're playing a six-line functional role, however). Try this: If you met your character at a party or on a long trip, how would you describe her to your delightfully cynical sister? The point, of course, is to find flaws the script really supports and that assist the telling of the tale.

LOSING CONTROL

Make room for the irrational (or the apparently irrational). I was watching a *Soprano*'s episode, and young Chris, Tony's nephew, was taking an acting class and doing a scene. The characters were using nonsense syllables to communicate, and after the first burst uttered by the other actor, Chris hauled off and knocked him down. Frustration apparently triggered it, and it was obviously impulsive. Impulse preceded thought or logic but in retrospect seemed completely in character, given earlier examples of Chris's hot head. Would your character ever lose control, and if so, would there be a slow build to the explosion or a trigger that releases an actor as a light switch illuminates a room? Naturally, losing control onstage is carefully contrived for everyone's safety, but if it happened in your play, where would it be and when?

THE PROBLEM WITH SEXY

God forbid you should have to play sexy because usually those who accept said assignment look sillier than hell. They twist their bodies in a knot, thrust this or that forward, shamefully intrude on the object's space, and generally behave as no one in the audience has ever seen a human behave before. Give us a break. Yes, we sometimes show ourselves off when we have something to show and a reason to show it, but remember our desire is to draw someone toward us, not put them off (or scare them to death). Remember that in most circumstances subtler is sexier. Sexy may be allowing the line of the body to attract, but it isn't burlesque. Sexy may simply be giving the other person your full attention and enjoying what he says and does. It may be a light touch on the arm—not a strip. It may be making eye contact just a moment too long, or sitting on the sofa with him instead of in the armchair. This is an area where a little underplaying will pay dividends. Leave something to the imagination.

THE DECATHLON

Think of the role as ten events:

1. Problem solving.
2. Working well with others.
3. Setting goals.
4. Self-knowledge.
5. Vulnerability.
6. Loving.
7. Ambitions.
8. Being centered.
9. Avoiding excess.
10. Unafraid.

Now decide which of these events your character is good at and which she sucks at. Let's say that you infer from the script that she's not very good at setting goals. Where, in what scene or scenes, is that playable in a way that illumines the text? Where is clear self-knowledge, or the lack of it, crucial to the character? What are her ambitions and how do they play out? By reading the text with this decathlon in mind, you'll begin to have a sense of the dimensions of the role. It's a way to begin.

THE INSIDE

THE EMOTIONAL RESPONSIBILITY

One of the most dismaying moments for the actor is when you read the script and find out you've got to break down on page 44 and find out about your mother's death on page 67. Just knowing you have to provide big emotional moments can shut you down. How do you prepare? There's that old favorite, substitution, where you use a deeply emotional memory from your own life (even if it has nothing to do with the play's situation) to trigger you at the key moment, or you can depend on a profound sense of the play's and character's circumstances to get you into the moment and imaginatively touch the emotional release button. Mainly, you have to free yourself from the idea of having to produce emotion. Your best recourse is the action. Focus on the action (what you want the other person to do, feel, or understand) and forget the emotion. If it comes, it comes; meanwhile you are fanatically focused on what the character wants and needs and whatever you do will be right. Remember that emotion is not the point, it's the by-product.

PASSIVE STATES

Yes, I know, there is a professional understanding that the best acting moves a passive state to an active one. However, let's examine for a moment the nature of this passive state. There is a substantial difference between not doing anything and preparing to do it. In acting, the useful passive state is one of using the moment to gather, prepare, and find the spiritual and physical balance to leap forward. States of constant activity tend to wear the audience out. Which is more dramatic—the swimmer who bounds up the tower to the high dive and forthwith leaps in the water, or the one who pauses at the edge of the board, needing the moment to vanquish fear, and, then prepared, dives? Look for those moments or sections where your character knows what she must do but needs time to generate the will to do it. There is immense activity in these moments even though they are quiet and still. One more thing, these moments open the door for that ancient but valuable theatrical device, suspense. Don't mistake a "gathering" state for a passive one.

VULNERABILITY

The actor must be affected by the circumstances and story in which he finds himself. He must first allow and then foster that vulnerability. In life we fight to defend our emotional vulnerability—to batten it, hide it, keep it out of the line of fire for fear others will ridicule or exploit it. In acting, to be overdefended in this way is brutally limiting and can make actors incapable of first-rate work and first-rate roles. You can't come to acting to hide; you must come to reveal. The hard part is that what *must* be and *is* revealed is often unattractive, weak, morally fragile, and deeply flawed. I know many fabulously talented people who simply cannot allow themselves to be seen in this light, and their work, with these faucets turned off, leaves us unaffected. You must open yourself to the role's journey and reveal your weakness and inability to deepen the flawed character. If you cannot, will you ever be more than workmanlike?

WRESTLING WITHIN

Some people live uncomplicated lives. They have clear goals, they pursue them sensibly, and then they achieve them. These people are not characters in plays. Characters also have goals, but they are conflicted, doubtful. They aren't sure how to go about it. They are continually reassessing their methods. The character second-guessing herself makes for wonderful acting opportunities. Look for the moments when the character is thinking, "I could do this or I could do that. If I do this, it might work out fabulously, but on the other hand it might really suck." The character's internal wrestling match about what to do and how to do it has, after all, given us *Romeo and Juliet*. Romeo, in the balcony scene, doesn't just set out to win Juliet and then win her. He worries he'll get killed by her relatives in the garden (even though he says the opposite). He worries she doesn't really love him. Should he propose? Maybe it's too soon? She questions his love—can even *he* be sure of it? Let's put it this way, Romeos who have absolutely no problem committing aren't very interesting Romeos.

YOUR LIFE AT YOUR FINGERTIPS

Your life is your main resource, so keep mining it. Having a hard time falling asleep? Impatient waiting in line to deposit your check? Trapped at a play so boring you could immolate yourself? Send the bucket down the well of your life. Usually you'll need a key word or image to start your time travel. Use hot button words like *anger, admiration, jealousy, longing.* Eagerly go on the journey your memory takes you. Investigate the circumstances and feelings that each word illicits. If you want an even more surprising but less-focused trip, use concrete nouns. Think of all the *chairs* you've sat in (no, I'm not crazy), the *barns,* the *grilled hamburgers,* and you will find yourself in parts of your life you haven't thought of in years. Your own life is your best acting tool. You need to know it so you can recall what is crucial for a certain role. Bring more of it back to a conscious level.

IMAGINED PERSONALIZATION

I wrote in *Tips I* about personalization. To remind, it's finding experiences in your life parallel to the one in the play that release your emotion and/or sense of what to do. What I didn't talk about was the role of imagination in personalization. Let's say that in the play you have a serious disagreement with your mother and ask her to leave your house. All right, let's say you haven't had that experience; your mother was a saint. Fine. However, what may illuminate the scene for you is the imaginary act of replacing (in your mind) the stage mother with your own. It may suddenly startle your interior life into a useful range of feelings that can inform the play. This form of personalization uses people you know as stand-ins for the other character to deepen your involvement and stimulate behavior. Put the image of someone you know in the scene. Interesting things may happen.

RELIVING

There is an actor's instinct to relive every piece of text that speaks about the past. We don't do it in life, and you shouldn't be overusing it onstage. Conduct this experiment for a day: Listen carefully to conversations and see how often there is real emotion-memory when the past is being referred to. A very small percentage of the time, right? Usually when we speak of our childhoods, we're not reliving them; we are bringing our experience to bear on a present problem. We are using the past illustratively not emotionally. Every once in a while, references to the past are emotional triggers—as are smells, images, tactile memory, and many other stimuli. But make sure the narrative demands it. Don't simply gild the memory with what you consider the requisite emotional tone. You don't necessarily have to sound sad because the line is about the death of a dog, or happy because you see a hummingbird. What's the character's present use of the past?

AMBIVALENCE

Sometimes the problem with a performance is that it's simply too clear, too single-minded, too black and white. Ambivalence can be a key dramatic tool. A lot of times we don't just choose option A. We start with A, give up too early; try B for a bit, and then go back to A. Would that life were a straight line from problem to solution, but usually it isn't. Worse, sometimes we're afraid to try anything, and we just sit there and stew. Look for the places in the scene where your character changes his mind rationally and emotionally. Look for the moment when he doubles back. Ambivalence often lets a breath of fresh air into an otherwise programmed character. Self-doubt allows the audience to wonder if there isn't more to the situation than meets the eye. Changing your mind isn't a passive state; it's moving from an active state to another (and perhaps back again). Hamlet's an immortal mess. You can be one too.

A SECRET LIFE

Someone—I completely forget who—said that every character has a secret life, and the character without one remains a simple construct. Yes, you must fulfill the necessities of the role but don't neglect the moment when we understand the handmaiden longs to be the queen. A supportive wife or husband might still have fantasies of escape and dreams of glory. The nerd wants to tango; the bully wants to raise flowers. Choosing a secret life for the character needs to take into account the play's structure. Nora, in *A Doll's House*, needs to be independent to find her true self, but at the same time she may have a secret dream of being a rich and powerful matron in an admiring society. Sometimes characters want to make the secret life known, and sometimes they struggle to distance themselves from the need. What is the secret life your character lives in daydreams and behind closed doors? Is there a moment in the play that reveals it, or a moment when she struggles to repress it?

PUSHING THE EMOTION

The actor recognizes that a given section of the text is "emotional," and while he doesn't inhabit said emotion, he is determined to provide it come hell or high water. He sobs loudly, beats the floor with his hands, shouts and rages and flings himself about. He is truly terrible. He doesn't believe it for a moment, but that doesn't stop him for a second. Stop worrying about the emotion. Cease. Desist. If the emotion isn't produced by the flow of the acting, the circumstances, your belief in the story, or some reference you find in your own life, don't provide a stem-winding alternative. Simply want what the character wants in the moment. Absolve yourself of the emotional responsibility. Forget what the script says you should do, as in: "He weeps, he tears his clothes, he eats the proscenium arch." Trust me, nothing is as unendurable as forced grand emotion. Better to do something simple and real. Don't cry, don't yell. Speak quietly and drop your wedding ring into her glass of water. Better to do nothing rather than the empty and large.

FREEDOM INSIDE STRUCTURE

Even in performance the actor needs to be free to manifest the impulse. However, the impulse must not destroy the structure. How can we have both impulse and structure? By structure, I mean the shape of the performance. Understanding where the character is now and where she will be soon. Knowing the points of the scenes, the actions that make the points clear, and the obstacles to those actions that reinforce the scene's energy. There are moments emotionally, physically, and vocally that we know must be there, but exactly how those moments look and sound are open to impulse. The presence of these defining moments and how they tell our story is the structure. The way they are filled is still open to impulse. Yes, of course, there are a few looks and sounds so carefully shaped that their repetition is demanded, but these tend to be few in comparison to the many moments to be played. Always know, in detail, what the telling of the story demands of you, but impulses that don't break the shape of the telling define the *living* stage.

THE PRIMEVAL OOZE

All right, come clean, what are you afraid of in the role emotionally? You decided to be an actor so you're going to have to get down in the muck. Where's the role's untrammeled sexuality? Where's the horrifying loss? Where's the uncontrollable paranoia, the petty, demeaning fear, the unattractive rage, the completely debilitating loneliness, the blazing narcissism? Are you sanitizing the role because something in you doesn't want to go there? Are you sort of halfway raging, sort of halfway lusting? When the primal is demanded, it's no good doing the cut-rate version. Today's the day. Cut it loose, throw yourself into it, let it consume you. This is why there have to be actors in the society. Someone has to tell the stories of the dark, the embarrassing, the extreme, the unmoderated—and you have signed on to do it. Don't put it off; it only gets harder. Yes, there may be foolishness and excess involved, but there is also enlightenment and the unforgettable. Go for it.

SILLY

You're often silly. I'm often silly. What about the character you're playing? It's particularly striking when a "serious" character gets silly. Now, what silly are we talking about here? I'm talking about the silly we want to have recognized as silly. I'm talking about singing a song that would be absurd in the circumstance. I'm talking about doing the soft-shoe in the rare book library. I'm talking about the silly hat, the outrageous Russian accent, the absurd imitation, the crossed eyes, the goofy walk. This sort of silly is often self-aware and even self-criticizing. It's often born out of the generous instinct to provide a laugh for someone who needs one or the necessity of making up for taking yourself too seriously. It can also be the perfect vehicle for creating the moment that needs inappropriate behavior. Any uses for silly in the role you're doing? The more dignified the character, the more striking silly becomes.

THE OTHER

DON'T PLAY WHAT THE OTHER ACTOR IS PLAYING

Unconsciously we sometimes fall in step with the other actor, particularly when he's good. I recently saw a *Glass Menagerie* where the gentleman caller seemed more sensitive and damaged than Laura and a *Look Back in Anger* where Jimmy's wife seemed angrier than he did. In comedy, I've seen an actor find a great bit of business in act 2, only to have another actor do it in act 1 in the next run-through. Sometimes it's a matter of picking up the tone, sometimes the manner, and sometimes the business. In any case, it tends to damage the point of the text or infuriate your colleagues. So much theater is dependent on opposites or differences. Romeo and Juliet are both in love, but they need differences in action and rhythm. When playing with wonderful actors, check whether you are unconsciously picking up some aspect of their performance. Bad guys aren't supposed to be just like the good guys. Celebrate your differences.

THE REACTION CHAIN

I've spoken about taking the time to see and hear the other actors and their intent. It is, however, the sustaining of this effort that gives your work its greatest power. Think of the work you are doing as a "reaction chain." The longer the chain is sustained, the more involving it becomes for the actor and the audience. I do something, you respond, I respond to your response, and so on. It has the growing fascination of a long volley in tennis. When the reaction chain isn't present, the work often seems precious or alienating. But remember, sustain, sustain, sustain. It's the cumulative effect that gives the acting heat. At this point, someone always says, "But what if the other actor isn't playing?" I would prefer to say, "Hit him upside the head with a serving tray," but the best you can really do is to heighten your response to what he is or isn't giving. Touch will sometimes wake up these somnolent actors. Talk to them about the scene. Lie and say you feel you're not giving them what they need. Open the communication.

TYING TONE AND RHYTHM
TO THE OTHER ACTOR

Not only do we need to vary tone and rhythm in our own work, we need to vary it *in relation to what the other actor is doing.* This is part of the active listening that so many trainers advocate. Now the disclaimer on this tip is that all tone and rhythm have an internal component, but for the moment I'm going to speak technically. Your tone and rhythm (note the biblical repetition) need to take into account what the actor speaking directly before you does. Many times I see (or rather hear) a series of exchanges on one musical note that shortly makes it impossible for the audience to follow the meaning. Same with rhythm. Don't steadily pick up a rhythm from another actor. Hear what she is doing and then vary yours. Actors are far too often solipsistic on this point. Remember, the net result of a steady beat or a steady sound is likely to lull rather than engage.

THE OTHER GUY'S SUBTEXT

We all know subtext is a valuable tool. What, after all, are we really saying? When another actor calls our work "interesting," we may ascribe many meanings, not all of them positive. Yes, exactly! You can find whole new colors in the scene by having your character interpret the other character's subtext and respond to it. For some reason we often feel subtext is only *our* province. Trying to follow another's subtext deepens our concentration, changes our response and reaction, and often changes our whole take on a scene. Paying this kind of attention really makes us listen. In life, we are always interpreting what others say to us. Career diplomats read between the lines and then act on their interpretations. If we are in the least suspicious or doubtful of the other's intentions, we comb their utterances for interior meanings. Because we are trained to want something from the other actor, we should listen carefully for what isn't said to increase our chances of getting what we want. The other actor's subtext often teaches us what to play.

HOW TO COMPLIMENT
ANOTHER ACTOR BACKSTAGE

A woman you worked with in a horrible production of *As You Like It* (played in an outdoor swimming pool) has given you tickets to see her as Laura in *Glass Menagerie*. You must go. You do. She's OK. Now you have to go backstage. Here's what you do. First, simply congratulate her. What an undertaking! A difficult role and she came through. She's looking at you shrewdly: What did you *really* think? Go backstage armed with specifics. Comment really clearly on three moments you particularly liked and why. All of us hunger for this kind of attention and very, very seldom get it. Once you've done that, switch over to a couple of questions on her process. How did she work on the limp? How did she develop her relationship with Amanda? The important thing here is that we all, most of all, want the intelligent and respectful attention of our peers, and you will have done that. You didn't say it was "interesting." You didn't generalize. You praised specifics and were interested in her process. Good job.

AND WHAT IS SHE DOING?

We are so aware, as actors, of our responsibility to *do* something that we sometimes overlook what's being done *to* us. Relax, breathe, give up your momentum for a bit, and fully take in what the other actor is doing. Now, react to what you're given. See how it forces you to adjust your action and tactics? Sometimes this "looking outward" takes an instant longer and, in fact, forces us to slow down and truly take in. Remember you are not simply "acting," you are acting in relationship to others. Remember that acting is a constant pattern of stimulus and then response. Go into today's rehearsal with a renewed resolve to hear and see through a quieted and centered spirit. Devote today to taking in; it will benefit all the tomorrows. It will refresh your work, stimulate others to make more contact with you, and deepen your involvement with the text, and by giving yourself away (so to speak), it oddly enough makes you more powerful.

OPENING THE OTHER PERSON UP

Ah, the gratitude you'll inspire! The director, currently thinking about his tax return, has left poor old Joey down left while you're way up by the bookcase. Not only that, but Joey is about to do his great speech about cobra venom. It's up to you to find a cogent reason (let's underline *cogent*) to move down on Joey's level or below. Good actors manipulate their blocking not only to improve their own visibility but to assist in positioning others for their big moments. Remember, these adjustments must not be baldly put. The move to give another actor the dominant position still needs to be psychologically sound. Often this give-and-take of the upstage or dominant position happens several times in a single scene. Some directors are aware of having left an actor in a closed position, and others aren't. Don't feel shy about solving such a situation yourself in a blocking rehearsal. It's not unusual and will be repaid.

HOW TO TALK ABOUT THE SCENE WITH ANOTHER ACTOR

First of all, think well of him. He is your colleague, you are mutually dependent, and he might have the solution to your problem on the tip of his tongue. Then remember we are all shy and clumsy and self-centered, so be gentle and sincerely interested and at least moderately self-effacing. Now:

1. Ask questions, don't make statements.
2. Phrase the conversation from the point of view that *you* have difficulties not that *he* does.
3. Try to develop and agree on a set of circumstances that surround the scene.
4. Don't sound piqued, dominating, officious, or like a street-corner know-it-all.
5. Start by asking him to help you with something.
6. Discuss the scene as if it were interesting not frustrating.
7. Listen!
8. Get a feel for his sense of the character's relationship.
9. Move the conversation delicately toward specifics.
10. End the conversation on a good note. Smile.

SIMPLE COURTESY

You doubtless have a cell phone. The stage manager doubtless has a cell phone. Get the stage manager's number. Now, always, always, always call the stage manager if you're likely to be even five minutes late to rehearsal. Always.

THE
DIRECTOR

SUSSING THE DIRECTOR

Lucky you, you just got cast in a new Theresa Rebeck play (lord, she must write one a week!) at the Denver Theatre Center. First day of rehearsal. Now who and what is this director? When working with a new (to you) director, pay close attention to her work in the first week. Her working style makes clear what you need to provide. If she blocks tightly, then your focus will be on internal work that makes her blocking yours. If she's a consulter ("Just move where you like"), then you need to be aware not only of your physical and behavioral instincts but how what you do juxtaposes with the other actors onstage *and* what it all looks like visually. If she focuses on the play's ideas, you need to find ways to communicate those ideas to the audience physically and textually. Each director leaves something for the actor to provide. Think of it as a doubles match with the director as a partner. Your process and your responsibilities vary given the director's strengths and proclivities. What will this director need from you? Watch closely.

CONTRIBUTE TO THE BLOCKING

As a director, I have a panoply of nightmares, but the one that most often comes true is the following: I'm blocking; the actors stare expectantly. They eye me with the passive disdain of a herd of Holsteins. I tell them where to go, and they go there. Then they eye me again. I block some more; the actors go there. It goes on forever. The good actor has ideas about the blocking. He often moves on the line before I say anything at all. The good actor stops me while I'm blocking and says, "Hey, what if I leave the book on the table and come back for it when I realize Helen might see it?" The good actor adjusts and moves up-right because he realizes he'll be in the way of the pattern I'm evolving. The good actor has ideas for behavior and use of props and how to fix the focus problems. If the director doesn't buy your idea, she'll tell you, but a high percentage of the time your instinct will prevail, and the director will be grateful. Save me from the nightmare; contribute.

WORKING WITH DIRECTORS

1. Befriend them; they're nervous.
2. They don't know everything. Don't expect them to.
3. Directors don't create *on* you; they create *with* you. Don't always wait for them; *do* something.
4. When you're not on, watch them. Sometimes you can only understand what directors want by watching them with others.
5. Good directors aren't asking you to do it now; they're asking you to work on it.
6. When you don't understand, say so (without hostility).
7. When you've been told to do one thing and want to try something else use the magic phrase "May I show you something?"
8. Really listen, it may be their subtext that's important.
9. Directors shouldn't make you feel foolish in front of your colleagues. That goes for you too.
10. Assume you're working with a good director until it's murderously clear you're not.
11. You won't know if an idea is right until you've given it your best shot. Try it twice without comment.

HOW TO BRING UP TEXT WITH THE DIRECTOR

On the simplest possible level, directors can't think of everything. Good directors know this. Monomaniacs are hostile to the idea. If you have an idea about what something means that seems to differ from what he is telling you, you have options. You could:

1. Say nothing and play the meaning you've discovered.
2. Phrase it as a question: "Is it possible this could mean _____?" Directors find questions less threatening than statements.
3. If you're very comfortable and consider him your friend or if he seems wonderfully undefensive, just say, "I don't think that's it. Isn't it _____?"

If your problem isn't a difference of opinion but quite simply incomprehension, the useful phrase would be "Can you help me understand this?" In any case, watch your tone. Try not to sound defensive, angry, depressed, or arrogant. Treat the director as you would a valued fishing guide. If she finds you irritating or unpleasant, she won't help you find the fish.

THE THREE BEATS IN
A TRANSITION

You remember the deal on transitions, don't you? A transition is the moment when the idea or subject changes for the actor as in, "So will you marry me? Are you all right?" That moment between the "me" and the "are" is the transition. Now that transition actually has three acting parts and they are: 1. Completion—the actor finishes one idea; 2. Reflection—the actor thinks what to say next; 3. Decision—the actor decides on a new course of action and speaks. All this could take place in a pause of some length, or it could happen in a split second. The important thing is that there is *process* in moving from one idea to the next. Too often the actor, knowing full well what the next line is, omits the steps that give a visibility to thought and turns speaking from something alive to something mechanical. Does every transition have three visible parts? God no. The big ones do. The others may be happening during the preceding line.

THINGS YOU DESERVE TO GET FROM THE DIRECTOR

1. Respect.
2. A good atmosphere.
3. A spirit of enquiry.
4. An interest in clarity.
5. A five-minute break each hour.
6. The possibility of repetition when you need it.
7. An understanding you may not be able to do everything "right now."
8. Five minutes of her time some time soon.
9. An answer to the question you asked yesterday.
10. A sense that you're engaged in a difficult profession.
11. The honesty to say when he doesn't know.
12. What the play's about.
13. What the scene's about.
14. An enlivening description of the situation.
15. A grasp of or at least a curiosity about the circumstances.
16. Some sense of what you're doing right as well as what you're doing wrong.

Will you get all these things? Sometimes.

WHAT YOU DON'T HAVE TO TAKE FROM A DIRECTOR

1. Anything you consider in the least dangerous deserves a conversation and careful rehearsal with sufficient repetition.

2. Sexual harassment. Don't put up with it. Call your agent, go see the producer. Call your union. Leave the area.

3. Demeaning comments about your acting that don't assist in making the work better. Request five minutes after rehearsal and tell him it's hurting your feelings and you don't like it.

4. Not giving your scenes sufficient rehearsal. Pleasantly ask for more.

5. Not taking care of it for you if you can't get the other actor to stop directing you.

6. Cutting your role in a serious way without consultation. Ask to discuss it. You may win or lose, but you get to talk.

7. General rudeness to you. She may not realize she's doing it. Ask for a meeting outside rehearsal.

THE DETAIL DEMON

There are directors who know or care as little about the actor's process as rocks or trees. They come in several flavors—these directors who make you wish you were dead. Today's flavor is the director who shuts down your creative process by micromanaging you early in the process. "No, no Arthur," says he. "Start the cross on the word *Excalibur*, sit on the word *aquamarine*, look at Amanda for two beats as soon as you sit, and then when she rises, cross your legs." Fun, huh? Dealing with such an obsessive is, of course, situational. If you know this demon, you can gently ask if he would let you explore some other possibilities. If you want to be extra careful not to offend, you can do as you're told and then slowly (not too much at once) explore. Most of the time the director won't insist on the original choice. If this methodology is really distressing you, ask for a meeting outside rehearsal and say you're enjoying the work, but you're not sure how to explore alternatives or contribute your ideas.

TOWER OF BABEL

What's the creative language being spoken on the production? There are so many training vocabularies and methodologies and highly personal semantics at play in the theater that the actor sometimes feels lost and confused. Is this a Stanislavski-based production? Meisner? Boleslavsky? Bogart? Suzuki? Spolin? Wilson? Brecht? The actor needs to pay special attention to the director's vocabulary during the first week of rehearsal. You may, for instance, be using the same words with different meanings. Don't be afraid to ask for clarification. Don't keep on using your vocabulary with her when it's plain she doesn't speak your lingo. If you feel simpatico with other cast members and they've worked with this director before, perhaps they can shed light over a cup of coffee. The key qualities here are trust and the desire to learn new tricks. Listen, ask, have faith. After all, what are the other options?

ASKING LATER

For the director, giving a note is a matter of timing. Will it be better heard now or tomorrow? For the actor, asking a question or giving an opinion is also a matter of timing. Very often it isn't so much about asking the director this or that, it's really a matter of getting your way, right? To accomplish this, you need to suss out the director's mood, and the mood of the rehearsal room generally. In my many years of directing, I've often been amazed by the actor's inability to recognize the wrong time to make her case. The director is harried and running late, has found out the lead needs to leave for a funeral, and just dropped his favorite coffee cup and smashed it to smithereens. The actor chooses this moment to suggest the director reblock act 2 because she's facing upstage too much. Seriously. When you have an important point to make in rehearsal, do it at a propitious moment, even if you have to wait a day or two. Sense the mood and the moment.

WORKING WITH THE BAD DIRECTOR

1. Disguise your opinion. Things are bad enough without her hating you.
2. Focus on the whys of the role. Usually a director would help you here, but . . .
3. Trust and follow your impulses, and don't wait to be told.
4. Think about how you fit into what the play means. Somebody has to think about the big picture.
5. Buddy up with your fellow actors so you can easily and valuably discuss the play.
6. Keep trying different things. You'll know what's best.
7. Try the horrible things he suggests, and then discard them bit by bit.
8. Say, "I might not get that right this minute," and then never get it.
9. Be polite and gracious and try to feed her ideas as if she thought of them.
10. Ask the best actor in the cast for tips.

THINGS NEVER TO SAY
TO A DIRECTOR

1. Complaining about another actor. Talk about the moment not the person.
2. "I don't have any idea what I'm doing." This insults the director who is working with you on the role. Speak in specifics not in generalities.
3. Overfamiliarity. Don't call him sweetie. Don't cling. Don't imply that you are great pals. Maintain a warm, friendly formality.
4. Don't say "I can't do that" until you've tried it more than once.
5. Don't say "My character wouldn't do that," or, worse, "My character wouldn't say that." It's not your character; it's the playwright's.
6. Before you disagree, ask for clarification.
7. Don't say you won't do that blocking. Do it, and then say "May I show you something else?"
8. It's dangerous to criticize the director to another actor. What if she passes it on?
9. Don't say "That isn't how I work."
10. Don't comment negatively on the production to the director. Duh.

THE AUDITION

AUDITIONING

There are several wonderful books on auditioning, but I've sat for so very long behind that table watching, well, maybe fifty thousand auditions, so I can't stop myself from adding my pittance to the pot. The most important thing, of course, is simply to do the work. Olympic athletes must out-prepare the others to win the gold, and so must you. The audition is the actor's version of a competitive sport. If you let someone out-prepare you, you either don't understand the situation or you secretly wish to fail. If you can put in three hours, put it in. Then you'll lose to the equally talented person who put in six. If anything, overdo your preparation. Many people more talented than you will be auditioning (yes, you are not the only fish in the sea). The good news is that the vast majority of these palpably more talented people are hopelessly, irremediably butt lazy. Want it? *Do the work.*

COLD READING

The question is, do you have overnight, or do you have ten minutes to prepare? For the sake of argument, I'm going to presume you have an hour.

1. If there's someone around, ask him for a quick précis of the whole script. If he is knowledgeable, ask for any info on your character. (Obviously, this is outside the audition room.)
2. Read the assigned scenes quickly, at least twice, for content, story, and meaning *without* making acting decisions.
3. Underline key moments, sentences, and words.
4. Determine what the character wants.
5. Determine what the character's expectations are in the scene.
6. Underline, in a different color, the major transitions.
7. Learn, if humanly possible, the first two lines and the last two lines.
8. Read it out loud at least three times trying different attacks and seeing where you can look away from the script.
9. Play for one or two big moments. Play for one or two big pauses.
10. When you do it, do it!

REALLY COLD READING

"Read this for us." Can I take it outside? "No, just read it for us now." Gulp.

1. Take thirty seconds to scan the page. If there's a long speech, glance over it—it will usually tell you what the major content of what you are reading is.
2. Hold the script below face level; they want to see you.
3. Run your thumb down the page as you read so you'll always know where you are.
4. Hit the first line with strong energy and strong emphasis. Same with the last line!
5. As you read the script, take a couple of pauses and during them memorize the shortest lines on the page so you can look off the text. Yes, it's possible.
6. If you're not being videotaped, move a little. It will build up your confidence.
7. If you make a mistake, don't look rueful, don't apologize, don't ask if you can go back. Keep going.
8. Use emphasis. Don't read flat.
9. Take an attitude toward the character and go full out.
10. Look as if you're enjoying it!

WHAT DIRECTORS LOOK FOR IN AN AUDITION

Well, certainly poise, charm, relaxed confidence, and a nice manner you'd like to be in a room with. The director always enjoys a sense that the actor is truly interested in the project (often, as protection, the actor treats the audition as something completely disposable). Anything the actor says in passing that allows me to believe the actor understands the play is a plus. Now, when the audition itself starts, I'm looking for good concentration, strong choices, a body that responds to the brain, emphasis in the line, whether or not the actor makes transitions, and a real sense of playing with the reader. I check in on the emotional intelligence and that hard-to-articulate sense that, given the role and the circumstances, I can trust the actor's taste. Does the actor have presence? Is the energy sufficient to deliver the role? Does she take adjustments? Is this a flexible spirit? Does she like to play? And has she put in the time?

AUDITION ZEN

Seriously, the biggest problem in auditions is being scared to death of them. Don't live your fear. Look outward not inward.

1. Find a newspaper article that reminds you there is more to life than acting. Carry it with you, and reread it while you're waiting.
2. Notice where you are. What color are the walls in the waiting room? How would you describe the actor across from you?
3. Remind yourself of four or five other things you need to do today. Concentrate for a moment on how you're going to get them done. Project in a practical way beyond the audition.
4. Accept your nerves. Everyone has them. They don't mean much. They don't define you.
5. Challenge yourself to itemize what all the people are wearing in the audition room. Take a moment to write down what they're wearing when you come out.

In other words, be aware of the details of the experience. It calms you and gives perspective.

AUDITIONING WITH STRONG CHOICES

Here's a surprising thing about auditioning professionally that I find most young actors don't know.
As a director, I don't usually end up with several
good choices. Usually only one person really stands
out for a role—on a rare occasion, two. That means
if you make strong, clear choices in your audition,
you have a chance. Most people play it safe. When
your powerful choice isn't what they are looking for,
you may go down in flames. But, on the other hand,
it may catapult you into contention. Don't be afraid
to take chances. Base your strong choice deeply in
the circumstances. Get your body into the scene. Let
them see you think on your feet. Then go for broke.
Your greatest competitive edge is the other auditioners' timidity. At the very least, it will mark you
as an actor to keep an eye on. Don't just say the lines
intelligently—want something desperately as the
character and show it.

AUDITION DON'TS

1. Don't talk endlessly about the strange thing that happened on the subway. They are on a schedule.
2. Don't come in for the callback if you have no intention of taking the part. It really pisses them off.
3. Don't try to pay the director compliments you don't really mean. It makes you look manipulative.
4. Don't do the whole audition sitting down. Show them you can move with intention.
5. Don't bring a lot of props or set a table for four. (Yes, I've seen that.)
6. Don't say, "I'll bet you don't remember me?" Just don't!
7. When you are given an adjustment, don't do the same thing you just did. (Yes, it happened to me twice today!)
8. Don't be rude to, manhandle, or sexually assault the reader.
9. Don't do the audition two feet from the director. Back off.
10. Don't wear eccentric clothing. We wonder why.

READ THE PLAY

Sometimes you find yourself giving audition advice that seems so obvious you feel simpleminded. How, one might ask, could you possibly impress with the scene if you haven't read the play? For instance, it might help to know that the person you're beating up is your brother! Doesn't everybody read the play? No. I came from a set of callbacks today, and I'd say 20 percent hadn't troubled to peruse the text. Why not? Well, often there's a bit of trouble involved. You might have to travel to someone's office to get one or visit a bookstore to find one. Sometimes it's a new play, and you would have to sit in the waiting room to read it. Allow me to say that the odds against being cast become, well, astronomical when you don't know the shape of the role. Whatever you have to do to get hold of that script, do it. Even if it didn't make you information-challenged to overlook this detail, it would still make the auditioners feel you don't really care. Believe me, we want you to care.

THE SECRET

Want to know what single audition failing is present in every actor I *don't* cast? They play every line in the same rhythm and often on the same musical note. This happens when an actor avoids deciding which lines are textually and situationally important by making all lines important. You see, if you were locked in a windowless room for eight hours (most audition rooms are, as you remember, windowless), would you want to pass the time listening to a metronome on one setting? Sometimes it actually feels like that. Thought has rhythms. Speech you would like to listen to has rhythms. Various rhythms. I've seen auditions that were all loud, all soft, all fast, or all slow, and I didn't cast a single one of those actors. The best acting is like watching a fire or listening to jazz. It isn't watching a obelisk or listening to a flatline buzz. Don't emphasize everything, don't yell everything, don't maintain a staccato. If you do, we won't cast you.

BE CLEAR, BE SIMPLE, DON'T SEEK TO OVERWHELM

That's it. That's the audition tip. After all these years of auditioning, I have to admit I get mighty tired of the overacting. I take it as a warning sign that the actor lacks taste, and to get a good performance from an actor whose taste is questionable is incredibly labor intensive for the director. We avoid such Herculean tasks when we can. An experienced director can measure your technique and emotional range without your making a fireworks display of it. Now, I'm not advising you to speak quietly in a monotone—but reveal the role, don't carve it like Mount Rushmore. Make clear the logic of what's being said (if it is logic). Allow the emotion to exist; don't wring it like a mop. Remember your auditors are probably (usually) intelligent and sensitive; don't spell it out as if to a child. If they like your work but are interested if you can enlarge, impassion, or double the ferocity, they will usually ask. I'm not saying work smaller; I'm just saying choose your spots for big.

AUDITION ATTITUDE

There's no way to outguess the people auditioning you; you can only commit fully to the work as you see it. Will they like you better blond? Would a casual offhandedness impress them? Who knows? Treat auditioning the way you treat performance. Develop your ideas. Take the material seriously. Spend adequate time. Find a logic in your choices inside the circumstances. And then, my friends, let it rip. Don't second-guess yourself while you're doing it. Study the text. Know the text. Don't play tone; play specifics. Pursue the action. If your work reveals the text and your auditors are aware, you'll have a good chance. Afterward, don't worry that you should have done this instead of that. Be proud that you made choices with the text as your guide and played those choices as if the world depended on it. If you have done that, you have done everything. If they don't like your interpretation, well, you can't control that. You have worked hard to play the text as you saw it. That's a good audition.

THE GOOD AUDITION PIECE

There's the search for the Holy Grail, the search for the Fountain of Youth, and the search for the great audition piece. What are its qualities?

1. You love it. It makes you laugh, it touches you, it speaks for you. You adore the writing. If the piece itself doesn't attract you, forget it.
2. You know what you do well. Is this a vehicle for you?
3. The situation in the piece is crystal clear within twenty seconds.
4. It has a strong present action. The character *needs* something. If it's a good story, there's a point beyond the narrative.
5. It allows for both movement and stillness.
6. It embodies some sort of passion.
7. It's a part you could play now, not fifteen years from now.
8. It isn't currently being overexposed. Nine other people won't do it the same day.
9. It's a piece that demands stage energy—mental, physical, or both.
10. You feel attractive doing it.

STUFF YOU CAN'T CONTROL

You auditioned; you didn't get the part. Stop doubting yourself. Here are some very possible reasons why you weren't cast.

1. You look like the director's ex-wife.
2. They prefer someone who comes dressed as the part.
3. They didn't like you coming dressed as the part.
4. The part was already cast.
5. They want someone who has played it before.
6. There aren't enough leads on your résumé.
7. You haven't played enough comedy.
8. They wanted a different look.
9. They wanted a different voice.
10. They loved you, but they took someone with more experience.
11. You're too tall for your love interest.
12. You're too short for your love interest.
13. They like actors with more technique.
14. They don't like actors with too much technique.
15. They've been auditioning for eight hours and hate all actors.

Don't take it personally.

AUDITION FOLLOW-UP

You did the audition and The Guthrie didn't want you for Edmund in *King Lear.* Now what? Well, the good news is they know you now. Keep it that way. Send the artistic director, director, and casting agent cards thanking them for the audition. Wish them well on the project, and express your wish to be seen for other productions. Send off these thank-you's within one week of being seen. If the director gave you an adjustment, thank her for working with you. If you know you will be visiting Minneapolis in the fall, ask if you may show them some other work at that time. Also make notes in your audition diary about who was in the room (be sure to listen if they introduce themselves to you), and jot down any pertinent information you gleaned during the audition. You may run into these people again in a different setting. Wouldn't it be nice to remember them?

THE THEATER'S CASTING AGENT

Most of the larger regional companies have someone on staff who organizes and has significant input into the theater's casting policies and calls. This person is separate from the New York or Los Angeles casting agent. If the theater is in Kansas City, she is a resident there, and while she will have other duties as well, casting is usually her most significant task. The theater's casting agent has the ear and respect of the artistic director and has probably been responsible for finding and hiring on a fee basis the casting agents the theater uses in New York and Los Angeles. Let's call her Rachel. Rachel arranges the coastal calls, chooses the audition studio, makes suggestions to the other casting personnel, brings in actors of her choice, and handles screening auditions when the artistic director absents himself. Get to know these people, stay in touch with them, and pay attention to them. All the power doesn't reside in New York.

AUDITION NOTATION

You come in; they hand you the sides (portions of the script to be read) and say they'll see you in fifteen minutes. What to do? Whip out your colored pencils and make the following notations.

1. Underline in red what you feel are the most important lines.
2. Put slash marks (/) where there are transitions to be made.
3. Circle key words you want to hit in blue.
4. Lightly mark through in yellow the lines you want to throw away.
5. Mark pauses you want to take with this symbol (V) in blue.

Now you could make up a dozen more marks for louder, softer, laugh, and so on, but keep it simple; you're an actor not a cryptographer. This takes practice. Pick up a book of audition pieces. Give yourself a limited time to mark one, and then get up and do it. Don't try this at a real audition until you've practiced at least a dozen times. Then go for it.

THE END OF THE AUDITION

You did it. You were great. Now, here's what you do.

1. If you feel it went well, you innocently ask if your auditors would "like to hear anything else?"
2. You say good-bye to people in the room by name. (Were you paying attention?)
3. You are particularly kind and polite to your reader.
4. You gather up *all* your stuff. It's uncool to come back for it.
5. You do not further engage those in the room in idle chitchat unless they initiate it.
6. You go outside the audition room and immediately write the particulars of the audition in your audition record book. Who was there? What were their titles? Was anything said you should note down?
7. You quiet your mind. You don't go over and over it. It's finished.

THE WORK NEEDS . . .

PLAYING LEADS

Yes, the size of the role isn't everything . . . but it's definitely something. You need to play some big roles to build your acting muscles. The big role gives the actor an experience of concentration, energy, complexity, and responsibility nothing else can. It teaches you to pace yourself, to seek variety, to accept yourself as interesting, to build the character's arc, and to deal with an emotional range no small part, however interesting, can match. The large part develops your analytical skills and your technique and timing. It forces you to discover where the big moments are and lets you feel the weight of others depending on your charisma. If you find you are steadily being cast in small or supporting roles, you need to take matters into your own hands and ensure your development by self-producing or calling in I.O.U.'s or being the squeaky wheel so you can have this crucial experience. Otherwise, when that big opportunity falls into your lap, you'll make mistakes you didn't need to make.

GETTING READY

Read this as sentimental if you will, but I do believe
that a life in the theater is a great privilege. Keep
that in mind as the day's work begins and progresses.
Any creative process has its irritations and any work
with human beings its annoyances, but remember,
having the job and doing the work is a state of grace.
Be there early. Settle into the atmosphere. Find a
way, be it meditation or your own form of center-
ing, to leave your other life at the door. Be patient
with others and the twists and turns of their
processes, and they are more likely to be patient with
yours. Remember that creative communication is far
from perfect, you may have to work to understand
what is being said to you, and even having understood, it may not work for you today but may fall
into place tomorrow. Patience. Grace under pressure.
Trust. These are transformative virtues for the actor.
The negative feelings of anger, self-dislike, and cruel
judgment make you forget your responsibility to a
creative atmosphere. Bring your best.

WHY IS IT ALWAYS "THEATER 101"?

The title of this tip is actually a humorously exasperated quote from the wonderful Seattle actor David Pichette during rehearsal. Why indeed? Why are we always forgetting stuff we know perfectly well about acting while we rehearse? I've always believed the actor and the chess master have much in common. There are so many layers of meaning, technique, and emotion that one can never keep them all in action at the same time. We're always working on one thing and forgetting another. This tip is simply, don't be too hard on yourself. You're never going to get it all. The role is always going to be, tantalizingly, a step ahead of you, and that's why we can never use it up, and the fascination and frustration of the work forever remains. When you get down on yourself and allow the illusion that nothing's right and you'll never get it and you're making one rookie mistake after another to take hold, you roadblock your own work. Relax. It's always going to be "Theater 101." Learn whatever it is for the hundredth time and move on.

WHAT'S FUN?

Acting has gotten to be a very serious business indeed. It has theories for this and vocabulary for that, text studies, movement structures from every corner of the globe, and all in all it seems more like theology every day. Remember this, you have to look forward to playing the role, not simply regard it as part of some endless doctorate. Before you immerse yourself in the psychology or deconstruction, sit down and tell yourself why it's going to be outrageous, creative fun to do this role! Well, for one thing, there's the fabulous mad scene in act 2! You get to mess with the conflicted love and affectionate hate of family relationships—and boy, do you have the background for that! You get to dance a short tango and kill someone with a broadsword and say that amazing speech about being fertilized by snake eggs! You get to wear an Armani suit and do a modified strip! Once you know it's going to be fun, you can face all the rest. Don't forget to recognize the role as a treat.

THE VETERAN RESOURCE

I recently directed a play that had two actors in their sixties and six actors thirty and under. What made my jaw drop were the social patterns in the green room. On one side of the room the two veteran actors chatted and on the other, the young Turks. This happened day after day, and I became more and more bemused. What were these young actors thinking? They seemed serious about their trade, they asked me questions in rehearsal, they wanted to learn (we were doing comedy and they seemed insecure about it), but they didn't seem to have a clue as to what these veteran actors had to offer. Acting is an oral tradition usually passed on through the medium of tales told of personal experience. The veterans know the answers to your problems, whatever they are. They have been there and done that. Engage the veteran actors! Pump them for stories, pepper them with questions, tell them your acting problems. They are the faculty of your graduate degree. Don't just sit there!

START SOMEWHERE

The rehearsal is over. You have one thought, one appraisal, one nightmare . . . you suck. Not only are you sure you suck, but you're pretty sure everyone else thinks so too. Agony and insecurity wash over you like a tidal wave. You could flee the country, commit ritual disembowelment, or go to work. For the sake of this tip, let's choose the latter. Our departure point is the simple idea that you can't fix everything. You will have to start with "something." Well, what's a big scene you hate? Turn to it. Pick a moment you're uncomfortable with and examine the circumstances that surround it. Hmmm. What is the action? What tactic might you use to accomplish it? Almost immediately an idea will strike you. Now pick a moment a few lines before or after the one you just worked on. After you've done three or four, you are likely to be teeming with ideas for the scene. Move to another scene and repeat the process. Move to a third scene. Now, that's enough for a night's work. Take those ideas into tomorrow's rehearsal. You'll feel refreshed and more confident. Light a candle; don't curse the darkness.

YOUR MORALITY AND ETHICS
AREN'T NECESSARILY THE ROLE'S

I worked for many years with an actor of remarkable temperament and skills. She was fabulous with text, wonderfully spontaneous, transparent emotionally, and highly skilled technically as well as transformative from role to role. She had only one problem—she was embarrassed by any scene that demanded her sexuality be engaged. "I just find all of that in such bad taste," she would say, and frankly she wouldn't represent it. I know another actor who opposed all forms of violent behavior and would not even slap another actor onstage. Do not accept roles or plays that you object to morally or ethically. The script shouldn't have to change (and usually can't) to accommodate your code. Once you have accepted the role, you have accepted the morals and ethics of the character. This is professional life. When you sense resistance in yourself, you must break through it. You are not the playwright.

WHY THIS SCENE?

This is for actors in training. Pick the scenes you use for class work carefully. I've had students say, "I'm always cast as the parent, never the love interest." So? Cast yourself as the love interest. Use your scene work to fill in gaps in your experience. Never played Shakespeare? Do the balcony scene. Never played low comedy? Do a dialogue scene from *A Funny Thing Happened on the Way to the Forum*. There are a few million books with scenes for young actors. Buy five or six or sit for a few hours in the bookstore. *Don't* waste your time by agreeing to do scenes you are not essentially interested in. These scenes should call to you; they should get you excited. This is one of the few areas where young actors can control their destinies. You need to do your research, find a dozen scenes and characters you would love to play, and even line up partners months before the class starts. You want to work with the best actors on roles you covet. If you aren't aggressive in this area, you have no right to complain later.

THE EQUITY CARD

The Equity card is your membership in the actors' union. It controls your working conditions and sets your wages in the professional theater. Do you want the card now? Maybe. Maybe not. Equity theaters may hire certain specified numbers of nonunion actors for significantly lower salaries, and they prize this arrangement given the eternal shortage of money in the American arts. Small parts and non-speaking roles are often given to cardless actors. If you are truly professionally competitive at this point and ready to earn your living in the business, then yes, you need the card. If you are preprofessional and learning your trade, you may want to retain your nonunion status and value to the theater as a budget saver. You may also be getting most of your crucial experience in non-Equity theaters where Equity actors may only be hired by special arrangement with the union. You don't need wings before you're ready to fly, or a card before you can successfully compete. Patience.

BE KIND TO . . . YOURSELF

I write this tip not to begin a self-help book but to make my own life easier as a director. I have often in my career experienced performers who waste their own time as well as others on the production by indulging in excessive (and public) worry or self-flagellation concerning their work. Of course, you're worried. Worry in our field is often a creative good. The point here is *how* your worry affects rehearsal both in terms of time and morale. Make sure you are not giving up. Try to keep your concentration on the problem you are working on rather than your subjective appraisal of your own abilities. I have heard actors say, "I just can't do this scene," and then set out to show they're right! Don't get in your own way. The moment when you realize the task's difficulty is the moment you begin to solve it. Plus, is it something we needed to know? To coin a phrase, "Suck it up."

GETTING DOWN

Dear actor, it's a tough profession. Treat yourself gently. Remember . . .

1. Eat, sleep, get out into nature. Laugh.
2. No, you're not bad in the role, you just had a bad day.
3. You can do it. Never, ever say you can't.
4. Treat yourself to a nice work area, good light, good paper, your favorite pens and pencils. Why shouldn't the actor have good tools?
5. Go to rehearsal looking good and wearing clothes you like.
6. Go out of your way to make friends in the cast.
7. All actors fear they will never be cast again. Of course you will. Dry periods are commonplace.
8. Really accept the compliments you get. You deserve them.
9. Enjoy your triumphs. Celebrate them. Give yourself presents.
10. Laugh at yourself. You're not a tragic figure.

STAMINA

I'm often surprised that many actors don't have the work ethic demanded by the profession. We know this work takes great energy and powerful concentration. Don't expect to be complimented for working hard; it's a given. Here are ten areas where that hard work is expected.

1. Learn the lines early—no ifs, ands, or buts.
2. Go over the blocking at home so you know it cold the day after it's been given.
3. When you get notes at the end of rehearsal, make the adjustment by the next day.
4. If you get line changes or cuts, they should be ready to go at the next rehearsal.
5. Your rehearsal energy and playing level should be as high at the end of the day as they were at the beginning.
6. You should play full out at techs unless instructed otherwise.
7. Don't wait until you're ready to play; play what you know now fully.
8. Stay at the required level, no matter how many repetitions.
9. Play or rehearse through colds, coughs, and minor illnesses without complaint or self-pity.
10. Stop whining and do it.

WHAT HAPPENED?

I'm obsessive enough to write down my rehearsal day. It may or may not be of use to you. At the end of rehearsal, I try to grab a quiet corner and do a five-minute take on the day's work. I ask myself only three specific questions. What worked? What didn't work? What did I learn? The trick, at least for me, lies in the specifics. I must not only say what worked but also what didn't work and why. I don't try to do an exhaustive job, just a few quick jottings. Under the "what I learned" category, I try to list things that I feel I can apply elsewhere in the script as well. What has proved useful about the habit is that because I write briefly, I tend to retain the ideas at least into the next day where they can serve as guidelines. At the end of each week, I reread the entries, which gives me a good sense of where I've stumbled without depressing myself. It keeps me from the dangerous, self-lacerating habit of generalizing about the work in a negative way. Don't let the rehearsal slip away.

NO-NO'S

THE TERMINAL CUTES

Ah yes, we all have our charms. In some of our performances, we have all too many of them. Recently I paid top ticket price to see a play where a young man came to his ex-sweetheart's apartment to make up after a large-scale relationship error. Oh, he was the very model of delicious, reticent rue. He stared at his feet, spoke sweetly and haltingly, cast his alienated partner melting glances, became tongue-tied, shuffled, and turned fetchingly pink. Who could resist him? He was a puppy in human form. I literally wanted to pet him. Then he redoubled those efforts. What began as ravishingly charming ended with my longing to drown him and the rest of his litter in a bucket of water. "Cute" in either sex can be audience-attracting but definitely in small servings and alternated with spicier fare. Don't overestimate the dose. Ask your director if you've gone over the edge. Maybe you should make this "cute" a tactic for getting a particular thing at a particular moment and not a staple of the characterization.

THE BAD ACTION

I see a simple mistake made over and over by actors when they choose an action. Don't develop an action at home that is dependent on something the other actor may or may not do. For instance, "I want her to stop crying." How do you know she'll *be* crying? Or, "I want him to stop being mean to me." Is that the only thing he can do with those lines? Whenever possible, the action you choose should not depend on the other actor's emotional state. You *can*, however, base an action on an emotional state you would like to *create* in the other, as in "I want her to finally feel free to be angry with me." Or, "I want him to express his love for me." Believe it or not, I actually heard one actor in rehearsal demand a specific emotional state from another actor! Why? He needed her in that state to play what he had decided to play. Worse, he demanded this state from an experienced actor with a notably bad temper. The rehearsal room was shortly an emotional bloodbath.

IDLING BETWEEN LINES

We've spoken about the actor whose face goes blank when it isn't his line. Watch the acting carefully in the next play you see, and you'll notice another variation of this. The actor speaking gestures heatedly while she talks. She pounds the table, she brushes back her hair, she points, she throws her hands up in mock horror. She is, all in all, a physical dynamo. Now she's not talking, she's listening, and lo and behold, she's a statue! What happened to gesture? What happened to behavior? In fact, where did her body go altogether? This actor's body is only engaged in the act of speaking, and all that means in terms of character and emphasis evaporates when she listens. Why? Does the body not engage in reaction? Do we never gesture at what we hear as well as accompanying what we say? Do we not continue to drink our milkshake while we listen? You see this odd dichotomy often in the actor who is not truly engaged in situation and circumstance. Just make sure your body stays alive more than 50 percent of the time.

EXPECTATIONS

You're a success! You did the role and everyone
loved you! Enjoy it, don't try to repeat it. Take in
the compliments, but don't work for the same ones
next time. "You were sexy and dangerous in *Richard
III*." Careful. Sexy and dangerous may be dead
wrong for the next role. You could even look . . .
well . . . foolish. As a young actor I had an antic
physicality that girlfriends and the unknowledgeable
tended to praise. Soon I was inserting lively physical eccentricities into roles as diverse as Loveborg
in *Hedda Gabbler* and Thomas Mendip in *The
Lady's Not for Burning*. I'd become a retrospective
exhibit, and I was only in my midtwenties. How did
it work? Very, very badly, thank you. And all in a
misguided attempt to generate the compliments I'd
gotten before. Make sure your work is devoted to
revealing the text not reprising your golden oldies.
You're too young to be Tony Bennett. You don't
want your acting to be a badly calibrated attempt
to attract a particular kind of attention you crave.
Of course, you won't do that because you're smarter
than I was.

ON FIRST SEEING
THE SET AND COSTUMES

Costume, set, sound, light, and prop designers have feelings. You would think we wouldn't need to talk about this, but allow me to reference two recent experiences. Experience one. I went into a tech rehearsal. The first time the leading lady appeared in her third-act costume, a strapless green cocktail dress, she made her entrance, peered into the house, and quipped, "I feel like a three-hundred-pound lime." Almost everyone laughed uproariously. Guess who didn't? The dress designer. Experience number two. I was in a fitting for a play about street kids, and as one of the young actors was given his costume to put on, he said, "My God, what's this supposed to be?" Designers are creative artists working for the good of the production. Bite your tongue. Don't sacrifice your relationship with a designer to get a cheap laugh. Phrase your reactions gently, if at all. Say what parts of the costume will assist you as a character and which might be a problem and why. Diplomacy rules.

BACK-TO-BACK

Remember tone? That's when you believe "humility" or "seduction" or "bitterness" has a special sound, and you use your idea of that sound to present "bitterness." Obviously not a good idea, but there is a specially virulent form of playing tone that can truly seem foolish. Let's call it emotional illustration.

SUELLEN: I am really, really unbelievably angry with you, George. You drive me crazy.

GEORGE: Sorry.

SUELLEN: You know I love you, why on earth would you do that?

The actor, seeing the word *angry*, adopts her "angry" tone and then immediately segues to her "love" tone when she runs into that word a line later. There is no emotional segue from one feeling to the other; she simply illustrates the words with sound. It's a kind of emotional shortcut that denudes the text of coherent reality.

FEAR FORMS

The actor keeps working in profile, and her long hair obscures her face. A mistake? No. She's doing it on purpose because she's afraid to be seen. The actor so overpaces the scene that it's almost impossible to follow. A failure of technique? No, he's scared, and he's hurrying to get the scene over with. The actor seems to have lost affect—not moving, not reacting. Forgotten a line? No, she's pretending not to be there at all. Unusual? No, it's present in a lot of actors who love the idea of acting but find the reality terrifying. Recognize something of this in yourself? (Been turning upstage a lot lately?) Or your classmate? Don't despair. It usually clears up as you understand the scene, the action, and the circumstances. Also, if you recognize the manifestations, it often disappears when you discard them. Stop hiding, and you realize nothing happens to you. Along with Churchill, I say we have nothing to fear but fear itself.

OH SO SAD

I recently saw a play concerning a man who comes home to discover his wife sleeping with a mutual friend. They were defensive, they hashed it out, they decided to split. Throughout, the husband and wife were deeply sad. Then they were sad some more. Finally, they *really* got sad. Dearest actor who reads these words, acting is the process of taking arms against a sea of troubles and, by opposing them, ends them. Take in the shock of the personal tragedy that afflicts and affects your character, and then soon, very soon, center your action around fighting your way out of the pit. Don't wallow! Among the awful things wallowing does to the actor is to drive him into a tone and often a passive physicality that does not move the play forward. Oh, it can be annoying! Sad is passive. Sad is self-regarding. Sad seems victimized. Sad is . . . well . . . boring. Concentrate your acting energy on what you must do, not how you feel. At the very least we want to see you fight to regain your balance. We respect the fighters.

HAMMY

No problem. We know we want to avoid being called this. So, what is it? It is usually thought to be acting scaled too large for the circumstances. It is particularly applied to drama in which the scale of emotions represented seems absurd rather than affecting. Hammy leaves nothing to the audience's imagination and seems self-consciously theatrical. Hammy is too much! Too much crying, too much rending of garments, too much angry behavior, too much being sexy, too much self-pity, too much extreme physicality . . . tooooooo muuuucchh. It is the theatrical version of showing off at a party. The reaction to hammy is "we get it, now stop." There are comic personalities in the theater who make a good thing out of hammy. They use the native absurdity of hammy to promote laughter. This kind of hammy is a talent and a gift, and very few comic actors have it. The size of a performance or a reaction is usually dictated by the circumstances, style, or genre.

STAGE FRIGHT

Stage fright normally occurs when you think about doing something in front of people. It usually disappears when you do it. Make sure that you see the first ten minutes of the play, or the act, as a series of simple tasks you know how to accomplish. If I tell you to go out in front of eight hundred people and tie your shoe, put the dishes away, and take out the garbage, stage fright abates. If I tell you to go out and be charming and then have a nervous breakdown, it increases. I repeat, break the first few minutes into tasks you know you can accomplish. After a few minutes onstage, it begins to feel normal, and sweaty palms dry. Drill the lines for the first ten minutes until you could say them in your sleep. Ask, in rehearsal, to make your first entrance several times. Give yourself a practical prop so you have something to do. Put things in your pockets to fiddle with. Go in with that untied shoelace and tie it. Create a beginning that feels normal and manageable. After that, you'll be fine.

THE SPECIAL PLACES
FOR SPECIAL SKILLS

You're a juggler? Good. You're double-jointed? Good. You play the tuba? Grand. Mastery of any skill is a fine thing. Just don't force it into the play for the hell of it! The special skill is best used in a play when it is a metaphor that reveals the story. Otherwise, it's just distracting. Sorry, I just came from a production where one actor in a relatively minor role in *Coriolanus* did a lot of (I'm not quite sure what to call it) . . . well . . . sword twirling. Why? I really couldn't tell you, but probably because he could. The next time I attend the International Sword Twirling Finals, I'll appreciate him. In *Coriolanus,* I just wanted to hit him with a rock.

HONESTY AND THE TRUTH: THE FETISH

OK, who can argue with honesty and truth? Every acting teacher celebrates them, parading them constantly like captives from a Roman victory. Directors speak solemnly of them as of heroes long dead. Actors pursue them without knowing quite what they're looking for. What do they mean, if anything? Usually they are a plea for the actor to remain recognizably within the parameters of circumstance, character, and plot. The danger is treating "honesty" and "truth" with the solemnity often associated with going to church. They often have the same effect on the actor as being shushed in the library. Everything suddenly gets very quiet and very small and very careful, draining the stage of sustaining energy. I'm not saying that's honesty and truth; I'm saying that's what happens when they are used as the bogeyman. My feeling is let's not talk about them any more. Let's pursue what we want from the other character within the circumstances and leave it at that.

BLUSTER

I was watching a well-known television actor audition for a play I was directing, and I was hating it. It was actually embarrassing! I found that while he went on, I was mainly staring at my shoes. What on earth was going on? He ran a gamut of emotions, he threw himself against the text, he shouted, he whispered, he gestured from head to toe. It should have been riveting, but it was in some perverse way absurdly funny. What was turning this wine to vinegar? It was showing off. He had skills, he had temperament, he (not the text) was going to overpower us, amaze us, knock our socks off! It was like watching a powerful locomotive plow across field and stream completely independent of the tracks. It was a hoot! We could dismiss the proceedings by simply saying it was melodramatic, but it was something worse. It was a talent broiling itself to death in self-absorption. Remember you are always partnering the text. Even when you're the only one onstage, acting isn't a solo.

SEVEN THINGS DIRECTORS HATE

1. They hate it when you don't write down notes at note sessions. Objectively, they want you to remember. Subjectively, they think you don't feel the notes are any good.

2. They hate it when you don't stay in the room for the complete run-through. Deep in their hearts they think you hate their work.

3. They really hate it when you sit in the tech and laugh at things that go wrong. I don't have to explain that, right?

4. They hate it when you want to have a long, serious conversation just when rehearsal has finished. Hey, they want to go home!

5. They hate it when you tell them about great productions you've seen of the play they're doing.

6. They hate it when you wear ugly, dirty clothes to rehearsal. Not only do they have to look at you all day, but they feel it's a commentary.

7. And they really, really hate it when you're late learning your lines.

Afterword

Be kind to yourself. In acting, as in chess, you rarely if ever find perfection. The actor is always a work-in-progress. There is always some moment in the play beyond our reach and some necessary skill we don't exel in. There's always something we know that we've momentarily forgotten, as well as situations we've never faced before where we are flying blind. Plus, damnit, we're all playing slightly flawed instruments. The trade's degree of difficulty is a big part of its fascination. The good news is you'll definitely get better through practice, and each decade of your work will bring new insights. Work hard and specifically, be patient, remind yourself of what you already know, and seek the next solution. Oh, and be kind to yourself.